www.colescookoff.com.au

First published in 2009

Copyright © Great Aussie Cook Off Pty Ltd 2009

All rights reserved. No part of this book may be reproduced or transmitted in any form or by any means, electronic, including photocopying, recording or by any information storage and retrieval system, without prior permission in writing from both the copyright holder and the publisher.

Big Sky Publishing Pty Ltd
PO Box 303
Newport, NSW, 2106
Australia

Phone: (61 2) 9918 2168
Fax: (61 2) 9918 2396
Email: info@bigskypublishing.com.au
Web: www.bigskypublishing.com.au

National Library of Australia Cataloguing-in-Publication entry

Title: Great Aussie Cook Off : Family Favourites.
Edition: 1st ed.
ISBN: 9780980325195 (pbk.)
Subjects: Cookery.
641.5

Cover and layout design: Think Productions
Typesetting: Think Productions
Printed in Australia by Ligare Pty Ltd

www.bigskypublishing.com.au

Notes for the Reader.

This book uses Metric measurements.

All spoon measurements are level.

See Resource section for full details.

Preparation and cooking times given are an approximate guide only.

CONTENTS

Fantasy Four 1

Knoll Family - The Butcher Boys 5

Soul Food 9

The Bui Family - 4 Spices 13

The Persian Cooks 17

Italian Maltesers 21

Campbell Family 25

The Lo Boys 29

Di Fulvio Family 33

Harwood Family 37

Cooks R Us 41

Inspired by Wine 45

Kitchen Witches 49

Thomas Family 53

Zuvela Family 57

The Quaffers 61

Team da'Husp 65

The Fighting Mongooses 69

CONTENTS

The Happy Café 73

Kay Family.. 77

Team Ados 81

Food Freaks... 85

Chiappin Family 89

Fechner Family 93

Kewco Queens 97

Team Bindass 101

Belle Italiani Family 105

The Super Storms.. 109

Cooking Calverts 113

The Campbell Cooking Crew 117

Groovy Grandmas.. 121

Eades Family 125

Macolino Family 129

Matinac Family 133

Pakwaan Group... 137

Resource Section... 141

INTRODUCTION

Australia has a wonderful diversity of culture, which has created our appetite for a wide range of fantastic cuisine.

Food is central to the Aussie lifestyle. It's the bond that brings friends and families together. Everyday around Australia, people from diverse backgrounds and cultural origins get together to cook their families' favourite recipes and experience the pleasure and enjoyment cooking brings.

The *Coles Great Aussie Cook Off, Family Favourites* cook book brings to you over 100 great tasting and simple to prepare recipes from the talented families of home cooks who entered the 2009, *Great Aussie Cook Off competition,* the latest reality TV series from the Nine Network.

Out of the thousands of entries received nationally, 35 families were selected and went head to head in a family cook off with heats held in each State. From these heats, eight families were chosen as finalists to compete on the TV series, The *Coles Great Aussie Cook Off*.

The *Coles Great Aussie Cook Off, Family Favourites* celebrates and showcases the culinary diversity, creative flair and passion of home cooks from all around Australia. In keeping with the "Family Favourites" theme, each family shares with you the inspiration behind their cooking style and the fabulously simple recipes they cook with passion and pride for family and friends.

To view videos of the teams cooking their recipes visit www.colescookoff.com.au

We hope you find this cook book inspirational and a valued and interesting addition to your cook book collection.

Image on Left:
Hosts Vince Sorrenti
and Jo Silvagni

NOW LETS COOK OFF

FANTASY FOUR

Our families come from a range of backgrounds covering all four corners of the globe including Poland, New Zealand, Greece, Indonesia, Ireland and the good, old-fashioned Aussie background.

Food has always been an important part of our families as it brings us all together, giving each person the opportunity to show their creative culinary talents. The importance of healthy eating is coupled with our desire to live an active life.

Dining with all our friends and families enables us to experience different cultures through the power of food and share the subtle differences each brings to the table.

Our cooking styles are simple, however, we love to experiment with new foods and recipes as well as developing different taste sensations. We are inspired by leading a healthy and active life and what's on the menu tends to mirror the emphasis we place on this.

Team Members: Lorinska Anderson, Kate Twigley, Mathew Seal, Andrew Merrington

ENTRÉE

YEAST FREE PIZZA
WITH HAM, GOATS CHEESE, ROCKET AND BASIL

★ Chooka's guilt free sensation

Preparation Time: 10 mins **Cooking Time:** 20 mins **Serves:** 2

STEP 1 Preheat the oven to 160°C.

STEP 2 Place the salt, olive oil and flour in a large mixing bowl, add water gradually while mixing together to make the dough.

STEP 3 Sprinkle some flour on a chopping board and your hands. Roll dough into a ball in your hands then place down on the board. Knead with the heel of the hand. Once the dough is smooth and elastic, either roll onto a round baking tray or, for thicker crust, spread with the heal of your hand.

STEP 4 On the uncooked pizza base spread tomato paste. Top with ham, followed by rocket and basil leaves, finishing off with goats cheese spread on top.

STEP 5 Once the pizza has toppings, glaze the edges of the pizza dough with olive oil. Place the pizza in the oven and cook for approximately 20 minutes.

Ingredients
200g plain flour
1 teaspoon salt
2 tablespoons olive oil
150ml water
tomato paste

Topping
100g ham
50g rocket
50g basil
100g goats cheese

HINT The tip to good dough is to not add too much water to the dough otherwise this can result in a sloppy pizza base.

MAIN

FILLET STEAK
WITH RED WINE, CHILLI & PARMESAN

★ Sealy's Speciality

Preparation Time: 10 mins   **Cooking Time:** 20 mins   **Serves:** 4

STEP 1 Grind black pepper coarsely on both sides of steaks. Heat butter in a large frying pan until brown, add steaks and cook over medium to high heat for 2–3 minutes on each side, or until cooked to your liking. Remove steaks from the pan and rest in a warm place.

STEP 2 Cook sweet potato in lightly salted boiling water for about 10 minutes, or until tender. Drain, add ground pepper, salt and butter (to taste) and milk and mash until smooth.

STEP 3 Add red wine to the frying pan and stir over medium heat for 2 minutes, scraping the residue from the base of pan.

STEP 4 Serve steak on top of mash. Pour sauce over steak and top with shaved parmesan and sliced chilli. Garnish with parsley leaves.

Ingredients
- 4 fillet steaks
- 2 large sweet potatoes (peeled and cut into pieces)
- 100ml red wine
- 4 teaspoons low fat milk
- 1 large chilli (finely sliced)
- 1 teaspoon parsley leaves to garnish
- small handful shaved parmesan
- black pepper (cracked/ground)
- butter
- salt and pepper to taste

DESSERT

GLUTEN FREE, LOW CARB PANCAKES

★ Cooking for the Models

Preparation Time: 5 mins   **Cooking Time:** 10 mins   **Serves:** 2

STEP 1 Mix flour, eggs, water, salt and sweetener together in a bowl.

STEP 2 Heat the frying pan and add a dash of oil (not required if using a non-stick frying pan).

STEP 3 Cook the pancakes until you can see air pockets rising on the surface then flip over to cook other side. Continue until all mixture is used.

STEP 4 Place shaved almonds under the grill for 1 minute to colour. Serve the pancakes with ice-cream, almonds and toppings of choice.

HINT The idea behind the Gluten Free, Low Carb Pancake is that it still has the yummy, fluffy pancake effect, but leaves out the unnecessary calories. These taste a lot nicer than the normal white pancakes and using the sparkling water makes such a difference, it adds extra fluffiness to the pancakes.

Ingredients

1 cup almond flour or gluten free self raising flour
2 eggs
¼ cup sparkling water
¼ teaspoon salt
1 tablespoon sweetener
2 tablespoon oil
banana
strawberry
roast shaved almonds
ice-cream
syrup/toppings

KNOLL FAMILY – THE BUTCHER BOYS

We are four brothers who have been around meat our entire lives. Our family has been making and selling German-style meat and smallgoods for the past 80 years, starting with our great, great uncle Andreas back in Bavaria, Germany in 1924.

We are all born and bred in Adelaide, however, have lived in Darwin and Sydney as Dad moved around with his work. Over that time, we learned to stick close together and to rely on each other – it was certainly easier than making new friends! We hang out together at work as well as after work to enjoy the simple things; good food, good drinks and good company.

Our cooking style is inspired by our Oma's (grandmother's) cooking – lots of pork roasts, rouladen, spaetzle (German noodles), soups and strudels appear on her table. We often make the trip up to the farm to take advantage of her cooking. We like to add a contemporary twist to our cooking. We call it modern meatatarian.

The whole family works long hours so getting together for a meal is one of the few times we get to relax so we take full advantage. Food for us is a simple pleasure and one that we can create ourselves. The preparation is all part of the fun, especially when things go wrong. Alex's most famous dishes are his Blue Lamb with fresh herbs and his Black Duck with Hoisin Sauce; both of which were a disaster but hilarious and have provided endless hours of torment over the years.

Team Members: Dieter, Stephan, Alexander, Andreas

ENTRÉE

SWISS BROWN MUSHROOMS
STUFFED WITH CARAMELISED ONIONS AND BLUE CHEESE

★ Yummy Mushies

Preparation Time: 5 mins **Cooking Time:** 13 mins **Serves:** 4

STEP 1 Preheat the oven to 180°C and line a baking tray with baking paper.

STEP 2 Cut the stems off the mushrooms and place open side up on baking paper. Cook in oven for 8 minutes.

STEP 3 Heat the oil in frying pan and add sugar, balsamic vinegar and onions. Stir together until soft and caramelised. Spoon even amounts of caramelised onion onto the mushrooms.

STEP 4 Divide gorgonzola into 4 pieces and place onto each mushroom. Place in a hot oven for 5 minutes and serve.

Ingredients
4 large swiss brown mushrooms
½ red onion
1 tablespoon brown sugar
1 tablespoon balsamic vinegar
50g gorgonzola cheese
baking paper
1 tablespoon olive oil

MAIN

SEASONED LAMB RACK
WITH FRIED POTATO CUBES AND A SALAD OF ROCKET, BEETROOT, FETA AND ROASTED PINE NUTS

★ Lamb Sensation

Preparation Time: 10 mins   **Cooking Time:** 20 mins   **Serves:** 2

STEP 1 Preheat oven to 180°C. Rub lamb racks with olive oil, salt, pepper, garlic, thyme and mixed herbs. Brown off in a frying pan for 2 minutes on each side. Place onto a baking dish and cook in the oven for 15–20 minutes. Let rest for 5 minutes before plating.

STEP 2 Peel potatoes and dice into roughly 2cm cubes and put into a pot with warm water and bring to the boil for 2 minutes before draining. Fry potato cubes in oil until golden brown. Drain and place onto paper towel to soak up the excess oil. Place potato cubes into bowl and season with thyme, sweet paprika, mixed herbs and salt to taste.

STEP 3 Place pine nuts onto a lined baking tray for 2 minutes or until brown. Dice the beetroot and place a handful of rocket onto each plate. Top with diced beetroot, crumbled feta and pine nuts.

STEP 4 Drizzle balsamic vinegar and a little olive oil over the salad. Add potatoes and lamb and serve.

Ingredients
- 4 desiree potatoes
- 2 x chop lamb racks
- 1 large tin baby beetroot
- 100g rocket
- 100g pine nuts
- 100g feta
- 2 teaspoons garlic paste
- 2 teaspoons balsamic vinegar
- 2 tablespoons olive oil
- 2 cups olive oil for frying
- salt and pepper
- dried thyme
- mixed herbs
- sweet paprika

HINT Test if olive oil is hot by dropping in one potato cube. If oil bubbles, it is ready.

DESSERT

STRAWBERRY PARFAIT
★ Stef's Strawberry Parfait

Preparation Time: 8 mins   **Cooking Time:** 20 mins   **Serves:** 4

STEP 1 In a bowl, combine the strawberries together with the brown and white sugar. Mix and allow to stand in the fridge for 20 minutes to release the strawberry juice.

STEP 2 In a separate bowl, mix the yoghurt, sour cream and orange rind.

STEP 3 Layer the strawberries and yogurt in parfait glasses, alternating between the two.

STEP 4 Decorate with mint and slivered almonds and serve straight away.

HINT Layer the strawberries thicker than the yogurt for a more elegant appearance.

Ingredients
2 punnets strawberries
¼ cup firmly packed brown sugar
4 teaspoons white or castor sugar
1 cup reduced fat Greek or natural yogurt
¼ cup lite sour cream
¼ cup grated orange or lemon rind
fresh mint for garnish
slivered almonds

SOUL FOOD

Our team is an intricate tapestry of the six degrees of separation. Georgie is our team captain, her brother in-law, Matt, is Simon's best friend. Matt's wife, Jo, is also Georgie's sister. Phew! Confused? Try saying that three times fast.

The bottom line is, we love cooking. Our cooking is inspired by love and laughter, fresh flavours, fresh food, exquisite taste and perpetual hunger. We love getting our kids and partners together for a great meal and a good laugh.

Georgie is a South Aussie mum of three little girls, and wife to the spunky Dale. She has been a food connoisseur from an early age. Jo has to feed two strapping sons and her larger than life bear of a husband. Matt is from Adelaide and definitely a meat and three veg sort of boy. He has gradually been broken in by his food loving wife to enjoy a wider range of food. Simon, a hilarious dad to two boys, and husband to the beautiful Jodie, is also from South Australia and comes from a family of fantastic cooks. So all up, we each bring something unique to the table and together make for a formidable cooking combination.

Team Members: Matt Hodge, Jo Hodge, Georgie Betterman, Simon Bowering

ENTRÉE

SPICED COCONUT PRAWNS

★ Mr Simon's Sexy Prawns

Preparation Time: 20 mins   **Cooking Time:** 8 mins   **Serves:** 4–6

STEP 1 Heat a non stick frying pan over a medium heat, add the lemongrass, chilli, ginger, garlic and oil. Cook stirring for 2 minutes or until fragrant.

STEP 2 Add the coconut and cook for 1 minute until toasted. Remove from the frying pan and set aside.

STEP 3 Clean the frying pan and add the prawns, salt and pepper. Cook for 2–3 minutes or until cooked through.

STEP 4 Return the coconut spice mix to the frying pan and toss with the prawns. Serve in a latte glass, lined with a serviette, with a lime wedge on top.

Ingredients
1kg green prawns (peeled, cleaned and tails left intact)
1 stalk lemongrass (very finely chopped)
1 tablespoon ginger (grated)
2 large mild red chillies (finely chopped)
2 cloves garlic (crushed)
1 tablespoon vegetable oil
3 tablespoons desiccated coconut
salt and pepper
lime wedges to serve

HINT Serve with a beautiful South Australian Sauvignon Blanc.

MAIN

CHAR GRILLED KANGAROO FILLET
DRIZZLED WITH A RED WINE AND CHILLI JAM GLAZE SERVED ON A BED OF MASHED NATIVE SWEET POTATO

★ A Very Pretty Man's Meal

Preparation Time: 20–30 mins   **Cooking Time:** 30 mins   **Serves:** 4

STEP 1 Marinate kangaroo in oil, salt and pepper for 20 minutes. On a very hot, oiled griddle plate, cook to your liking, making sure all sides of the meat are seared. Once cooked, move onto a plate to rest and cover with foil.

STEP 2 Cook potatoes in salted water until tender. Drain, mash and add in cream, cumin, vegetable stock, salt and pepper.

STEP 3 For the glaze, cook all ingredients together over a medium heat for about 10 minutes until slightly reduced.

STEP 4 Slice the kangaroo diagonally and place on top of the creamy mash, drizzled with glaze. Garnish with some coriander and fresh sliced chilli. Serve with a side salad or steamed veggies.

Ingredients
- 4 kangaroo fillet steaks
- 1 organic sweet potato
- 4 small potatoes
- 4 tablespoons cream
- 1 teaspoon vegetable stock
- olive oil
- ground cumin to taste
- salt to taste
- pepper to taste

Red wine and chilli jam glaze
- 50g butter
- ½ cup red wine
- ½ cup beef stock
- 2 tablespoons chilli jam or red currant jelly
- sea salt and cracked black pepper

HINT This goes well with a Cabernet Sauvignon in winter, and in summer try a chilled Rosé – delightful.

DESSERT

BUSH HONEY CHOCOLATE FONDUE
WITH TEMPTATION SPEARS

★ Jo Jo's Fave

Preparation Time: 15 mins   **Cooking Time:** 5–8 mins   **Serves:** Varies depending on quantity of dips selected

STEP 1 Dice all the fruit into chunks and thread onto skewers.

STEP 2 Melt cream and chocolate carefully over a hot water bath until smooth.

STEP 3 Add in the honey and pour into a fondue bowl.

STEP 4 Dip the skewered fruit and other ingredients into chocolate and devour.

Ingredients
350g chocolate
¼ cup bush honey
¼ cup pouring cream
2 bananas
1 punnet strawberries
1 punnet fresh raspberries
½ cup honeycomb
½ cup marshmallows
2 kiwi fruit
1 orange
1 packet thick wooden skewers
½ cup pretzels
½ cup dried fruit

HINT The 'temptation' is stopping at one! You can try making a separate fondue platter for the kids with mixed lollies as well. For the adults, you can add a good slug of Kaluha or Baileys.

THE BUI FAMILY – 4 SPICES

There are five girls in our family and no boys. Our Dad is the luckiest man on earth! Our team is made up of four of the five girls.

In 1981, our parents escaped war-ravaged Vietnam. Forty-five family members, consisting of aunties, uncles, brothers, sisters, great uncle, great aunts and cousins all squeezed onto a small fishing boat and headed out to sea. Not knowing where they were going or whether they were going to survive the rough seas, they lived on what rations they had. After nine long days at sea with hardly any rest and no food we finally came across land. This new land was called the Philippines. We stayed there in refugee camps for two years before we were sponsored to come to Australia; a great country which we now call 'home'.

Tanya and Chrisii were both born in Vietnam. Michelle was born in the refugee camp in the Philippines and Linda was born in Australia along with our baby sister, Sabrina. We have been in Melbourne ever since.

Early on, dinner was always the same; it consisted of either a fish or meat dish with stir fry vegetables and a watery soup of some sort. As we got older, food and dinner time became more adventurous and precious. All of us would get together once a week at our parents house. Mum would always cook up really traditional Vietnamese cuisine, such as 'Pho' which is Vietnamese beef noodles or her famous 'Bun Bo Hue', known as chilli beef and rice noodle soup. Our cooking is inspired by our Asian background and our Mother's traditional Vietnamese cuisine.

We love cooking as it brings our families together and it allows us to gas bag about how lazy the men in our lives are!

Team Members:
Michelle, Tanya,
Linda, Chrisii

ENTRÉE

VIETNAMESE SPRING ROLLS

★ Spring Rolls

Preparation Time: 15 mins   **Cooking Time:** 5 mins   **Serves:** 4

STEP 1 Place noodles and dried fungus into separate heatproof bowls. Cover with boiling water. Stand for 5 minutes. Drain. Roughly chop.

STEP 2 Combine noodles, mince, dried fungus, diced carrots, garlic, onions, fish sauce, sugar, salt and pepper into a bowl. Mix well.

STEP 3 Separate the spring roll wrapper into individual pieces and place on plate. With a spring roll wrapper edge facing towards you (so it looks like a diamond shape on the plate), place 1 teaspoon of mince mixture along one corner of wrapper closest to you. Fold in the two sides, and roll making sure the wrapper is nice and tight as you roll. Brush the end with a little bit of oil to seal. Place onto a tray. Repeat until mix is finished.

STEP 4 Half fill a wok with oil. Heat on medium to high heat until hot. Cook spring rolls in batches; cooking for 5 minutes, or until light golden. Remove to a wire rack.

STEP 5 To make chilli dipping sauce. Combine chilli, garlic, sugar, water and lemon juice together and stir until sugar is dissolved.

STEP 6 Serve the spring rolls with lettuce, mint leaves (optional) and chilli dipping sauce.

HINT The tighter the rolling of the spring roll the crunchier the spring roll will be. Do not have the oil too high as this will burn the spring roll wrapper and not fully cook the mince mixture inside. Do not over fill the spring roll with too much mixture as it will be harder to roll plus longer to cook.

Ingredients

50g bean thread vermicelli noodles
200g pork mince
2 garlic cloves (finely chopped)
1 onion (thinly sliced)
1 carrot (diced into small pieces)
½ cup dried fungus (mushroom)
1 tablespoon fish sauce
2 cups hot water
1 tablespoon caster sugar
1 teaspoon salt
pinch pepper
12 round spring roll wrappers
peanut oil (for cooking)
¼ iceburg lettuce
mint leaves (optional)

Dipping sauce
1 small red chilli (finely chopped)
1 clove garlic (crushed)
1 tablespoon sugar
3 tablespoons water
½ lemon (juiced)
thinly sliced chilli to garnish (optional)

MAIN

WON TON NOODLE SOUP

★ Yellow Noodle Soup

Preparation Time: 10 mins **Cooking Time:** 20 mins **Serves:** 4

STEP 1 Bring stock and ginger to the boil in a large saucepan over high heat and then reduce to a simmer while making wontons.

STEP 2 To make wontons; place bean thread vermicelli noodles in a small, heatproof bowl. Cover with boiling water. Stand for 5 minutes. Drain and roughly chop. Place pork, onion, cabbage leaves, vermicelli noodles, sugar, salt and pepper in a bowl. Mix until well combined.

STEP 3 Place 1 wonton wrapper on a clean surface. Place 1 heaped teaspoon of pork mixture in the centre. Fold up all four corners of wonton wrapper into the centre and twist to enclose filling and form a little money bag. Press to join. Repeat using remaining wrappers and pork mixture. Set aside.

STEP 4 Bring a large saucepan of water to the boil then reduce heat to medium. Cook wontons in water, in batches, for 3–4 minutes or until pork is cooked through. Remove to a bowl using a slotted spoon. Cover to keep warm. Then in the same pot, add the egg noodles and cook for a few minutes until the noodles separate and are cooked through. Drain well and set aside.

STEP 5 Just before serving, separate the lettuce leaves and place at the bottom of each bowl. Place egg noodles on top of the lettuce with the BBQ pork (optional) and then divide the wontons between each of the serving bowls. Ladle over stock and sprinkle with spring onion and serve.

Ingredients
2 cups chicken stock
1cm piece ginger (peeled and thinly sliced)
4 small iceberg lettuce leaves (halved)
1 sprig spring onion (thinly sliced)
egg noodles
bean shoots
BBQ pork (Cha Siew) optional

Wontons
200g pork mince
½ onion (finely chopped)
1 tablespoon caster sugar
50g bean thread vermicelli noodle
2 Chinese cabbage leaves (finely chopped)
pinch pepper
½ teaspoon salt
24 wonton wrappers

HINT The wontons can also be served on their own. You can tell when the wonton is cooked by watching it rise to the top of the pot when cooking. The wonton wrapper also changes into a transparent colour. You can deep fry the wontons instead of boiling them.

DESSERT

CARAMELISED BANANA CREPES

★ Banana Crepes

Preparation Time: 10 mins **Cooking Time:** 10 mins **Serves:** 2

STEP 1 Add flour, icing sugar, salt, egg and milk into a mixing bowl. Mix with a whisk until combined. Melt unsalted butter in a frying pan over a medium heat and add to the crepe mixture. Stir until butter has disappeared into mixture.

STEP 2 Heat a crepe pan, or non-stick pan, on low heat. Add a small amount of crepe mixture into the pan. Swirl mixture to create a thin circle layer. Cook the crepe for 1 minute on each side. Transfer to a plate.

STEP 3 Over a medium heat add the banana and sugar. Wait until sugar caramelises and the banana changes into a bright yellow colour.

STEP 4 Fold crepes in half and then in half again. Place in centre of serving plate. Top each crepe with caramelised banana. Drizzle with maple syrup and serve with a scoop of ice-cream (optional).

Ingredients
- 1 cup plain flour
- 2 tablespoons icing sugar
- 25g unsalted butter
- 2 eggs
- 250ml milk
- 4 tablespoons sugar
- pinch salt
- 2 small bananas (peeled and thickly sliced diagonally)
- ice-cream to serve (optional)

HINT You can also use other fruit in this dish instead of bananas. Don't over-fill the pan with batter. Crepes are supposed to be nice and thin. You can add a few drops of water to the sugar when caramelising to help the process along if the sugar is not dissolving.

THE PERSIAN COOKS

Our passion for cooking comes from our rich culture. Our parents originate from the beautiful city of Shiraz in Iran. We all came to Australia over 24 years ago.

Our family foundation has always been very strong, and family meals have always been extremely important in bringing everyone together.

The Iranian traditions and culture have certainly stayed alive in our family. This can clearly be seen in our rich, colourful, not to mention delicious meals. My mother makes every meal from scratch using the freshest produce, meat, chicken, fish and of course beautiful Iranian herbs, spices and nuts.

Our family's passion for cooking has always brought us together and sometimes has caused confusion in the kitchen as family members come up with new suggestions; especially when we as a couple disagree about the way food has to be prepared. This leads to new experiences. Some of the more traditional dishes that we prepare sometimes take Grandpa and Grandma back to places far from home.

Canned and frozen foods are a definite 'no no' in our home; unless we are trapped underground and can't escape for another three months. Freshness is definitely important to the flavour and texture of our meals.

Team Members: Sahel Ashktorab, Bahar Jamshidi, Farhad Ashktorab, Sanaa Ashktorab

ENTRÉE

YOGHURT & CUCUMBER DIP
★ Sahel's dip

Preparation Time: 3 mins   **Cooking Time:** 2 mins   **Serves:** 4

STEP 1 Peel the cucumber (if it is not a Lebanese cucumber, try to take out the seeds as they can cause the dip to go watery).

STEP 2 Once peeled, grate the cucumber and drain any excess water.

STEP 3 Add the yoghurt and stir until thoroughly mixed. Add mint and dill, reserving a teaspoon of mint for decoration. Add salt and pepper and mix thoroughly. Decorate with mint.

HINT Enjoy the dip with some crispy bread sticks.

Ingredients
1 Lebanese cucumber peeled
6 tablespoons natural yoghurt (preferably Greek style)
1 teaspoon fresh dill (chopped)
3 teaspoons dried mint
salt and pepper to taste
bread sticks to dip

BARBERRY RICE (ZERESHK POLO)

★ Farhad's Polo

Preparation Time: 10 mins   **Cooking Time:** 20 mins   **Serves:** 4

STEP 1 Soak rice and add cooking salt and leave for at least 2 hours. Bring half pot of water to boil and add soaked rice. Allow to cook for at least 6–7 minutes or until rice is semi hard. Drain and wash with cold water. Place pot over stove on low and pour 1 tablespoon of olive oil. Pour the drained/washed rice into the pot. Mix a pinch of saffron with olive oil and 2 tablespoons of boiling water and pour evenly over the rice. Cover with aluminium foil and close the lid. Allow the rice to cook for about 15 minutes before serving.

STEP 2 Cut each chicken fillet into four pieces. Place 20g of butter in a frying pan and allow to melt. Add chicken pieces and cook until golden brown.

STEP 3 To make the saffron sauce mix; in a bowl place the remaining saffron, juice of 1 lemon, tomato paste and 1 tablespoon of boiling water. Add salt and pepper to taste.

STEP 4 Add saffron sauce mix to the chicken in the frying pan and bring to the boil. Once boiled, turn the heat to low and allow fillets to slowly cook in the sauce. Turn the fillets occasionally while waiting for the rice to cook.

STEP 5 Prepare the barberries 5 minutes before serving rice. Place 20g of butter in a frying pan and allow to melt. Drain barberries and add to melted butter. Stir and add a little saffron. Add sugar and mix until the sugar is melted and barberries have a glossy red colour.

STEP 6 Serve rice with the barberries on top and garnished with slivered pistachios. Place the chicken next to the rice and pour over the saffron sauce.

Ingredients
3 chicken fillets
1½ cups basmati rice
2 tablespoons cooking salt
50g barberries
2 tablespoons slivered pistachio nuts or silvered almonds
1g saffron (ground)
1 lemon
1 teaspoon tomato paste
2 tablespoons olive oil
50g butter
2 tablespoons white sugar
salt and pepper to taste

HINT Don't overcook the rice otherwise it will break into little pieces.

DESSERT

PERSIAN CREAMY DELIGHT

★ Bahar's signature

Preparation Time: 10 mins | **Cooking Time:** 15 mins | **Serves:** 4

STEP 1 Pre heat the oven to 180°C. Beat egg whites until stiff and add the sugar. Beat until the sugar is thoroughly dissolved and egg whites are glossy. Add vanilla essence to the egg yolks. One at a time, add egg yolks to egg white mixture and beat until mixed. Sift flour and baking powder into the mixture and fold in with a spatula.

STEP 2 Place baking paper onto a baking tray. Spoon mixture into a piping bag with a flat nozzle and pipe the mixture into the tray, roughly the shape and size of soup spoon. Make sure the mixture is not too close to each other. Place tray in the oven for 15 minutes or until biscuits are a light golden brown. Allow to cool.

STEP 3 Pour cream into a bowl; add icing sugar and rose water. Beat cream with an electric beater until peaks form. Pour cream into piping bag with star shaped nozzle.

STEP 4 Hold two pieces of the sponge biscuits in the palm of your cupped hand with the tops facing out (flat side on the inside). Make sure the base touches each other and pipe cream in three straight rows one after the other. Place on a serving tray and garnish with crushed pistachio nuts.

Ingredients
- 100g flour
- 75g white sugar
- 3 eggs separated
- 1½ tablespoon baking powder
- 10 tablespoons icing sugar
- 250ml thickened cream
- 2 tablespoon rose water
- 1 teaspoon vanilla essence
- 1 tablespoon crushed pistachio nuts

HINT Before serving refrigerate for at least 15 minutes. When sponge biscuits are cooked remove immediately from the cooking tray to avoid hardening.

ITALIAN MALTESERS

My grandparents grew up in Calabria and my parents are from Arena and Ariola, Italy. Dad, Michael Daniele, came to Australia in 1955 and my mother, Angela Daniele, followed in 1957.

Dad inspired our family by growing up and working in and around fresh produce. He didn't come, see and conquer but rather he came, saw and concreted! He doesn't believe in having plants or animals that don't produce food. The family home was not surrounded by flowerbeds or cuddly pets, instead there were vegetables, fruit trees, 36 chickens and 14 roosters who all bear the name 'Jack'.

My mother Angela is the homemaker who not only prepares and creates fine Italian dishes for the family, she also makes jams, pickles and homemade sauces from the produce Dad grows in his garden. The family now extends to a third generation and Dad makes Italian bread in his backyard oven and Angela continues to prepare meals for everyone.

My parents are living examples of past generations as demonstrated by their parents, Francesco and Maria Antonia Daniele, and Fioramante and Costanza Costa. These are our ancestors whom we have to thank for our inspirational cooking.

As we say, "There's nothing better than homemade pasta!"

Team Members: Frank Daniele, Angela Daniele, Angela Barbara, Michaella Barbara

ENTRÉE

HOMEMADE ITALIAN BRUSCHETTA

★ Pane Papa (Dad's Bread)

Preparation Time: 30 mins   **Cooking Time:** 60 mins   **Serves:** 2

STEP 1 Pre heat oven to 200°C (fan forced).

STEP 2 To make the bread mix all of the ingredients together by hand in a large bowl. Gradually sprinkle in the last of the flour to get a nice mixture of dough. Cover the mixture with a tea towel and leave for approximately 25 minutes to allow the dough to rise.

STEP 3 Once the dough has risen, remove from the bowl and place on a chopping board sprinkled with flour. Using your hands, fold the dough over until the dough is a nice texture. If the dough becomes too sticky add some more flour until it is soft but not dry.

STEP 4 Sprinkle some flour on a clean tea towel. Remove the dough from the chopping board and wrap in the tea towel. Leave the dough for approximately 10–15 minutes to rest.

STEP 5 Once the dough has been rested, place it on a pizza tray sprinkled with flour. Bake in the in the oven at 200°C for approximately 1 hour or until the bread is golden brown. Take the bread out of the oven and let it sit for 10 minutes.

STEP 6 Take 2 slices of bread and drizzle olive oil on one side of each piece. Heat a grill pan and grill bread on each side until golden brown.

STEP 7 Top with alternate slices of bocconcini and tomato and garnish with torn strips of fresh basil.

Ingredients

Homemade Bread
3 cups plain flour
1 tablespoon dry yeast
½ tablespoon salt
2 cups warm water
extra flour for kneading

Topping
2 slices truss tomato
4–6 slices bocconcini
basil to garnish
olive oil

HINT Making homemade Italian bread has been passed down through the generations. A variety of toppings can be used but we like to use the ones in this recipe.

MAIN

FUSILLINI
WITH FRESH TOMATO SAUCE AND CANNELLINI BEANS

★ Custom Creation from Past Generations

Preparation Time: 5 mins **Cooking Time:** 20 mins **Serves:** 4

STEP 1 To prepare the fresh tomato sauce. Wash and cut the tomatoes into halves and boil in a pot until soft. Strain the tomatoes in a colander to reduce the water, and then blend into a pure tomato sauce. Cook the olive oil, garlic and onions together in a pan until brown. (Add parsley, basil and/or oregano if desired). Add the blended tomato sauce to the other ingredients in the pot and boil for ½–1 hour until the sauce becomes thick.

STEP 2 Cook the pasta in a pot of boiling salted water for approximately 10–15 minutes until al dente. Just before draining pasta, add broccoli and cook for 2–3 minutes, or until cooked. Drain the pasta and broccoli and return to pot.

STEP 3 Heat the pasta sauce in separate pot. Add the beans and stir until heated through.

STEP 4 Add the beans and tomato sauce to pasta and serve with shredded parmesan for topping.

Ingredients
1 x 500g packet San Remo Fusillini
1 x 400g can cannellini beans
1 bunch broccoli
salt to taste
shaved parmesan for topping
Fresh Italian Tomato Sauce
1kg bag ripe tomatoes
½ onion (chopped)
1 clove garlic
fresh parsley, basil or oregano (optional)

HINT While cooking this dish, taste test regularly to ensure it is to your taste and add a little extra of whatever your taste buds desire.

DESSERT

ITALIAN AFFOGATO
★ Meta Meta (Half and half)

Preparation Time: 2 mins   **Cooking Time:** 10 mins   **Serves:** 2

STEP 1 Percolate the coffee. Add between 1–2 cups of water to the coffee, depending on the size of the percolator.

STEP 2 Put 1 scoop of ice-cream in a serving dish.

STEP 3 Once the coffee is ready; mix in 1–2 teaspoons of sugar.

STEP 4 Pour the coffee over the ice-cream and decorate with the mint leaves and wafer. Serve.

HINT It is an Italian tradition is to have an Italian espresso coffee after a large meal. We have incorporated the dessert and coffee together.

Ingredients
2 tablespoons espresso coffee
1 large scoop vanilla ice-cream
1 wafer
3 mint leaves
1–2 teaspoons sugar

24

CAMPBELL FAMILY

Both Meredith and Bryce descend from British ancestry. Meredith is a country girl at heart, growing up in Bathurst, New South Wales, while Bryce spent his early years on a small farm just outside Coff's Harbour. Our children Hayden and Harley are able to boast about living by the sea as we now reside on the northern beaches of Sydney.

Our parents and grandparents were people who cooked and served good, wholesome homemade meals. A number of signature dishes have been passed through the family over the generations and these always make their way to the dinner table on large family gatherings.

We draw our cooking inspiration from our appreciation of good food and the joy of sharing the occasion with friends. There is no particular style to our cooking; we will have a crack at anything, if it looks good, we will cook it. We have found all our favourite dishes are from recipes we have developed ourselves.

Team Members: Meredith Ripley, Hayden, Harley, Bryce Campbell

ENTRÉE

SAUTÉED ASPARAGUS
WITH POACHED EGG, PROSCIUTTO AND SHAVED PARMESAN

★ Asparagus Sensation

Preparation Time: 5 mins **Cooking Time:** 12 mins **Serves:** 1

STEP 1 Trim asparagus spears to a consistent length. Blanche the asparagus for 40 seconds.

STEP 2 Heat oil in pan and sauté asparagus and prosciutto on medium heat.

STEP 3 Break the egg into a cup lined with cling wrap. Remove the cling wrap and twist the top and secure with an elastic band. Place wrapped egg in boiling water and poach the egg for 3 minutes.

STEP 4 Place the asparagus on a plate. Cover with roughly chopped crisped prosciutto. Place the poached egg on top and garnish with shaved parmesan and pepper. Dress the plate with vinaigrette.

HINT Use the asparagus water to poach the egg.

Ingredients
5 asparagus spears
1 egg
2 rashers prosciutto
shaved parmesan
1 dessert spoon olive oil
fresh ground black pepper
Vinaigrette
1 teaspoon parsley
1 teaspoon basil
olive oil
vinegar

MAIN

CRUMBED FISH FILLETS
WITH TARTARE SAUCE, DRY ROASTED POTATO SCALLOPS, WILTED BABY SPINACH AND ROAST TOMATOES

★ The Captain's Special

Preparation Time: 10 mins   **Cooking Time:** 25 mins   **Serves:** 1

STEP 1 Preheat oven to 220°C. Peel and slice the potato (approximately 6 mm thickness). Place on an oven tray, brush with olive oil and season with salt and pepper. Bake until golden brown on the outside and tender on the inside.

STEP 2 Dust the fish pieces in flour, dip in egg, and roll in panko. Place in the fridge till required.

STEP 3 On a sheet of foil, place some olive oil, Italian herbs, garlic and tomato halves and roast for 15 minutes.

STEP 4 Prepare the tartare sauce by combining mayonnaise, sour cream, lemongrass, coriander, cornichons, capers, lemon juice and pepper to taste.

STEP 5 In a frying pan, heat the vegetable oil and fry fish pieces until golden brown.

STEP 6 In another pan, wilt the spinach with a couple of drops of both sesame oil and olive oil. Plate up the fish and serve with the spinach, tomatoes, roasted potatoes and tartare sauce.

HINT Fry the fish until moisture starts to weep from fish. Panko is Japanese bread crumbs available at most supermarkets.

Ingredients
4 small fish pieces (flathead, snapper or barramundi)
1 cup panko (Japanese breadcrumbs)
1 egg (beaten)
1 large potato
¼ cup baby spinach (washed)
1 medium tomato (halved)
sesame oil
vegetable oil (to shallow fry)
garlic and Italian herbs
olive oil
sea salt and fresh ground pepper
flour for dusting

Tartare Sauce
2 tablespoons mayonnaise
1 tablespoon sour cream
½ teaspoon lemongrass
½ teaspoon coriander
1 dessert spoon each chopped cornichons and capers
lemon juice to taste
pepper to taste

DESSERT

CARAMELISED BANANAS
WITH BRANDIED SAUCE, CHOCOLATE PECANS AND CREAM

★ Fabulous Banana Surprise

Preparation Time: 10 mins   **Cooking Time:** 5 mins   **Serves:** 1

STEP 1 Melt the dark chocolate in the microwave on medium heat for 30 seconds, repeat until melted. Dip the pecan halves half way into the melted chocolate and place on baking paper. Sprinkle with sea salt and refrigerate till required.

STEP 2 Melt the butter in a frying pan. Add the sliced banana and sauté until bananas start to go soft.

STEP 3 Sprinkle the brown sugar over the top of the banana and toss to incorporate. Cook the banana and sugar mixture until the sugar caramelises.

STEP 4 Add the brandy to the mix and flame up. By tossing the bananas in the pan the brandy will flame up from the burner flame. On an electric appliance you will need to ignite with a match.

STEP 5 Serve with a good dollop of cream and garnish with the chocolate pecans.

Ingredients
1 banana (sliced)
6 pecan nuts (halved)
50g dark chocolate
2 tablespoons dark brown sugar
25g butter
40mls brandy
sea salt
dollop double thickened cream

HINT The salt adds a pleasurable dimension to the chocolate. Stand at arm's length when the brandy flames, unless you are sick of your eyebrows.

THE LO BOYS

Our cooking is inspired by our very interesting and multicultural family. Dad was born in Sabah, Malaysia 40 years ago. His father is Malaysian Chinese and his mother Australian. "Gong-gong", our Chinese grandfather, loves to cook, and not just Chinese food, but Aussie cakes, pavlovas, the whole lot! He is a fantastic cook and taught his great recipes to our Dad and now Dad is teaching them to us. The best thing about Asian food is you get to try lots of different meals and flavours at the one sitting.

Our paternal great grandparents, who were born in China, were farmers who kept pigs and chickens and grew vegetables to sell at the local market. Grandma's father was a dairy farmer from Lismore and our Grandma grew fabulous veggies and strawberries on a small hobby farm on the outskirts of Sydney when Dad was a boy.

It's not surprising that, not only do we enjoy cooking, but we also enjoy growing and catching our own food. As well as fishing, we have a friend with a small farm at Freeman's Reach who slaughters his own sheep and cattle and also grows awesome veggies. He gives us lots of ingredients and it doesn't get fresher than that!

I guess you'd say our cooking style is a fusion of East and West, with a heavy Eastern influence. All of our dishes are a mix of handed down recipes and our own variations. We love to cook together as it's something everyone can do and we have lots of fun in the kitchen. We don't get invited to lots of places because there are so many of us, but lots of people come to us to try our tasty creations!

Team Members:
Tom, David, Josh, Ben, Sam (front)

ENTRÉE

STIR FRIED KING PRAWNS IN GARLIC AND GINGER

★ Gong-gong's King Prawns

Preparation Time: 10 mins **Cooking Time:** 2 mins **Serves:** 1

STEP 1 Peel, de-vein and butterfly the prawns, leaving tails intact.

STEP 2 Heat half of the vegetable oil in wok until hot. Add the prawns and stir-fry for 30 seconds until they have changed to an orange colour, but are still slightly translucent. Remove from the wok with a slotted spoon and set aside.

STEP 3 Add the remaining oil to the wok and add sugar snaps, fresh ginger and garlic for 30 seconds. Return the prawns to the wok with wine, vinegar, soy sauce, sugar and sesame oil and stir-fry for 30 seconds.

STEP 4 Serve immediately with steamed jasmine rice.

HINT To test if the oil in the wok is hot enough to start your stir-fry, place the end of a wooden chopstick in your oil as it is heating. When the oil around the end of the chopstick starts to produce small bubbles the oil is at its optimum heat for stir-frying.

Ingredients

6 green king prawns
8 sugar snap peas
1 teaspoon white sugar
1 tablespoon vegetable oil
4 slices fresh ginger (chopped or grated)
1 teaspoon garlic (crushed)
1 tablespoon Shao Xing wine
2 teaspoons malt vinegar
2 teaspoons light soy sauce
1 teaspoon sesame oil
1 tablespoon water

CHINESE FISH SOUP WITH NOODLES

★ Jia Ting (meaning 'family') Soup

Preparation Time: 15 mins **Cooking Time:** 10 mins **Serves:** 1

STEP 1 Pour vegetable oil into a deep, heavy based frying pan and lightly fry the ginger and chilli on a medium heat.

STEP 2 Add the fish stock to the pan and stir until simmering. Gently place the fish in the simmering stock and cook for 2–3 minutes, until the fish is translucent in the middle and soft white on the outside.

STEP 3 Add the noodles. After 2–3 minutes add bok choy, mushrooms and spring onion. Simmer for a further 5 minutes.

STEP 4 Remove from heat and place in shallow bowl. Heat sesame oil in separate saucepan until smoking. Pour over soup and sprinkle coriander to serve.

HINT Do not allow the stock to boil as it will cook the fish too quickly and become tough. Remember the fish will keep on cooking in the soup after you take it off the heat.

Ingredients

1 fillet of any firm white fish (The Lo Boys recommend Wide Mouth Nannagai from North Queensland)
50g noodles (udon or soba)
1 tablespoon vegetable oil
4 slices fresh ginger
½ teaspoon chilli paste
1 small bunch bok choy (end removed but leaving the leaves whole)
1 handful Enoki or Shitake mushrooms (sliced)
1 spring onion (julienned)
375ml Campbell's fish stock
1 tablespoon light soy sauce
1 tablespoon sesame oil
1 tablespoon fresh coriander (roughly chopped)

DESSERT

STEAMED COCONUT CUSTARDS WITH LIME

★ Grandma's Po Po Custards

Preparation Time: 5 mins **Cooking Time:** 15–20 mins **Serves:** 2

STEP 1 Place the coconut milk, cream, caster sugar and egg yolks in a bowl and whisk to combine.

STEP 2 Gently stir the lime rind through mixture.

STEP 3 Pour the mixture into 2 ramekins and place into a bamboo steamer. Steam over boiling water for 6–8 minutes (or until just beginning to set).

STEP 4 Allow the custard to stand for 5 minutes to cool and set further before serving. Serve with a slice of fresh lime to squeeze on top of the custard.

Ingredients
½ cup coconut milk
½ cup cream
2 tablespoons caster sugar
2 egg yolks
1 teaspoon finely grated lime rind

HINT Refrigerate the custards for 10 minutes to help them set.

DI FULVIO FAMILY

Our inspiration for cooking comes from our heritage. Our Italian parents originate from the Abruzzo Region on the Adriatic Coast. They arrived here over 50 years ago. We've been raised with their fondness, appreciation and love of great tasting food and wine.

Growing up, we thought it was normal to make all your own 'stuff'. Our upbringing with food has been based on a lot of simple, home made food and hanging around the back yard watching our parents and grandparents make the home made pasta, tomato sauce, pork sausages, sardines, roast capsicums and tomatoes (even cut up the odd cow, lamb, goat, pig, duck, chicken etc). Our kids have been a part of this now so hopefully the next generation will not lose the culture.

I suppose our family loves cooking together because it's one way to catch up with each other on the day's events and also get a say in what we will have for dinner or help prepare for a special family get together. Most of the time we all get involved (and sometimes argue) about what, and how much we'll cook.

If it's not fresh forget it! If its soup out of a can you could be stoned, if the spaghetti sauce is not tasty, you have failed dismally...Only joking of course!

Team Members:
Eda, Will, Tom, Frank

ENTRÉE

PRAWNS WITH CHILLI AND GINGER ON CIABATTA TOAST

★ Eda's Spicy Chilli Prawns

Preparation Time: 5–8 mins **Cooking Time:** 10 mins **Serves:** 4

STEP 1 Heat half a cup of olive oil in a large frying pan. Crack a little sea salt and pepper into the oil. Add chilli, frying until just sizzling. Add the prawns and when they start to turn pink, add the garlic and ginger.

STEP 2 Toss all remaining ingredients around in the frying pan, making sure prawns are well coated in oil, garlic and ginger. Cook for approximately 4–5 minutes, or until the prawns are cooked. Make sure the garlic does not start to overcook. At the last minute mix in one teaspoon of extra chilli powder or Italian mixed spices.

STEP 3 Grind in sea salt and pepper (more or less to taste). Switch off heat and allow to sit while you lightly toast the bread. Break the bread into mouth size pieces and place on a small plate. Evenly distribute the prawns and oil mixture per person over the bread. The ciabatta soaks up the juices.

Ingredients
½ cup extra virgin olive oil
1 thumb size piece fresh ginger (cut into thin strips)
3 large garlic cloves (chopped)
2–3 fresh chillies (sliced into rings)
whole large peeled prawns (approximately 8 per person)
cracked sea salt and pepper
chilli powder
Italian mixed spices
ciabatta bread (toasted)

HINT Oil should be hot before adding in the ingredients, don't overcook the garlic and use enough salt and pepper otherwise the taste is bland.

MAIN

VEAL INVOLTINI
★ Frank's Incredible Involtini

Preparation Time: 10 mins   **Cooking Time:** 10–15 mins   **Serves:** 4

STEP 1 Beat the egg and mix in parsley and cheeses. Season with salt and pepper. Add 2 cloves chopped garlic, set aside.

STEP 2 Heat oil in a medium frying pan. Add red onion, fry for 2–3 minutes and then add tomatoes. Cook for another 2–3 minutes. Add 1 finely chopped garlic clove and add salt and pepper to taste. Reduce heat – don't overcook garlic. Set aside.

STEP 3 Flatten veal pieces and season with cracked sea salt and pepper. Spread parsley and cheese mix thinly onto half veal steak. Roll the Involtini over from parsley side, slightly tucking in each end to avoid cheese coming out. Lightly cover the Involtini in corn flour. Set aside.

STEP 4 Heat oil in another medium frying pan. Cook the Involtini on slow to medium heat until light brown. Add tomato mix and finish cooking together. Once the meat is cooked, transfer to a serving plate and use tomato as topping. Serve with fresh, crusty bread rolls.

Ingredients
10 small sized pieces veal topside (approx 100mm x 130mm) lightly tenderised
½ cup extra virgin olive oil
1 egg
½ cup corn flour
1 cup Italian parsley (very finely chopped)
1 cup grated parmesan cheese
1 cup grated Romano cheese
3 cloves Italian garlic (very finely chopped)
1 roma tomato (chopped)
½ red onion (finely chopped)
sea salt and black pepper
fresh, crusty bread rolls

HINT Add more cheese to the egg mix according to taste: it should have more of a cheese flavour than parsley. Cook Involtinis slowly otherwise they will not cook evenly.

DESSERT

TIRAMISU
★ Tommas' Tantalising Tiramisu

Preparation Time: 10 mins   **Cooking Time:** 15 mins   **Serves:** 4

STEP 1 Beat egg whites until stiff and set aside. In another bowl beat egg yolks and sugar for 3–4 minutes or until smooth.

STEP 2 Add softened Philadelphia cream cheese and beat for 30 seconds. Add thickened cream and continue beating for 30 seconds. The mixture should be thick and smooth. Add egg whites to egg yolk mixture and beat until peaks form.

STEP 3 Dunk biscuits in coffee and marsala mixture and arrange a layer into 35x30x4cm dish. Cover with half the cream mixture. Sprinkle with crumbled Flake. Repeat with another layer. Refrigerate, serve and enjoy.

HINT Make sure coffee is cold before dunking. Don't over dunk biscuits as they will go soggy and cream will be runny. Make sure the cream mixture is stiff and beaten well before spooning into dish otherwise it will not set. Tiramisu is best when its left for at least 2 hours in the fridge to set.

Ingredients
- 3 free range eggs (separated)
- 3 tablespoons caster sugar
- 250g Philadelphia cream cheese (softened)
- 600ml thickened cream
- 500g pack Italian Savoiardi biscuits (Ladyfinger)
- 6 cups freshly brewed espresso coffee, sweetened and cooled
- 1½ cups Marsala Liquor
- 2 x 45g Flake chocolate bars

HARWOOD FAMILY

I grew up in a place and time where olives were considered exotic. In the 1960s, Bunbury, Western Australia, was just seeing the introduction of 'strange foods' such as capsicums and rockmelons.

My husband and I wanted to bring our children up in the country, so we started to look at businesses and thought egg farming looked easy (I didn't say we were smart!). In 1992, we purchased a small caged egg facility and over the next few years converted it to free range, with the goal of converting to organic.

Our children, Max, Kelly and David showed as much interest in cooking as in any sandpit or new experience. The children have grown up on the farm and are accustomed to the rigours and peculiarities of that life; although none of them want to be a farmer, they have an appreciation of fresh food.

Since moving to the farm in Margaret River, we have had a constant stream of overseas visitors and workers staying with us. All are very keen to show off their culture and repay our hospitality by cooking for us. Through this and our own travel, we have been influenced by a wide variety of sources in both our cuisine and life. Our cooking is definitely multicultural and I think we'd try almost anything once!

Eating and preparing food has always been an activity that our family has enjoyed. It has always brought us together as a family.

Team Members: David, Kelly, Jan, Max

ENTRÉE

VIETNAMESE ROLLS
★ Rice Rolls

Preparation Time: 15 mins **Cooking Time:** 10 mins **Serves:** 4

STEP 1 Mix all the dry ingredients with the wet ingredients together thoroughly.

STEP 2 Place one rice paper sheet at a time into a bowl of very warm water. Soak for 30 seconds or until the paper begins to soften. Remove paper from water and lie flat on chopping board.

STEP 3 Place a large spoonful of mixture on the end of the rice paper, fold the sides of the paper in and then roll up the rest of the paper around the mixture so that you end up with a tight shape. Serve with dipping sauce.

HINT Many different varieties of vegetables and meat can be substituted depending on what is at hand or is best and freshest. Change the size of the rice paper to suit the purpose, i.e. large for dinner or small for hors d'œuvre.

Ingredients
Dry Ingredients
12 rice paper roll sheets
1 cup shredded cooked chicken (can be poached, roasted or bbq)
4 cups finely shredded fresh vegetables - cabbage, carrot, cucumber, capsicum, spring onion
½ cup chopped fresh mint and coriander
¼ cup bean shoots and/or rice vermicelli
12 large cooked and peeled Australian prawns (optional)

Wet Ingredients
50g canned tuna with tomato and onion or similar or 1 tablespoon fish sauce
1 teaspoon sesame oil
1 teaspoon soya sauce
1 tablespoon sweet chilli sauce
1 tablespoon lemon or lime juice

Dipping Sauce
¼ cup white rice or wine vinegar
1 teaspoon sweet chilli sauce
1 tablespoon chopped peanuts

MAIN

MEDITERRANEAN FISH AND VEGETABLES

★ Max's Fish Dish

Preparation Time: 15 mins **Cooking Time:** 10 mins **Serves:** 4

STEP 1 Lightly fry the onion and tomato in some olive oil. Add the wine (stock or water may also be used) and boil for 1 minute to reduce the liquid. Mix in the lemon juice and chilli (to taste) and season with a little crushed garlic. Place the mixture on four individual aluminium foil squares and top with a little basil. Add the fish and fold up into an enclosed envelope.

STEP 2 Cook the foiled envelopes with the tomato side facing down on a barbeque or frying pan on low heat for 5 minutes or until fish is white through. Open the foil to check the fish while cooking, as exact cooking time will depend on the thickness of the fish. With this recipe it is also okay to overcook the fish slightly without drying it out.

STEP 3 While the fish is cooking, cover a saucepan with 2cm of water and bring to the boil. Add the prepared vegetables. Cook on high for 3 minutes, or until just 'al dente'. Drain the vegetables, return to the pan and toss with olive oil and citrus juice.

STEP 4 Heat some extra olive oil and the butter in a frying pan over a low heat until the butter has melted. Add the crushed garlic and breadcrumbs and cook until crisp. Sprinkle over the vegetables.

STEP 5 Serve the fish with the seasonal vegetables and garnish with lemon and chilli slices.

HINT One to impress the girls.

Ingredients

4 x 200g white firm fish fillet
2 tomatoes (diced)
1 onion (diced)
1 cup water (or stock or white wine)
4 tablespoons fresh lemon juice (or orange or lime)
400g each of fresh green beans and broccolini (or asparagus if Mum is paying)
1 cup fresh breadcrumbs
4 teaspoons butter
2 cloves garlic
fresh basil
salt and pepper to taste
1 tablespoon olive oil
1 tablespoon of citrus juice (mixture of lemon, lime, orange)
chilli to taste
extra garlic for seasoning
extra lemon juice, lemon slices and sliced chilli for garnish
olive oil for frying

DESSERT

SEASONAL STEWED FRUIT

★ Lilly on the Pond

Preparation Time: 10 mins　　**Cooking Time:** 8 mins　　**Serves:** 1

STEP 1 Peel, core and cut the pear into 4 sections lengthwise. Sprinkle with sugar and spice. Microwave for 1–1½ minutes on high. Set aside.

STEP 2 Mix milk, cornflour, egg, sugar and vanilla extract together and stir over a low heat until just thickened.

STEP 3 Finely dice the dried fruit and mix into the ice-cream. Put into a cling wrapped cup or mould and refreeze until firm.

STEP 4 Invert the ice-cream into the middle of the stewed fruit and serve with the custard. Garnish with glace ginger or shaved chocolate.

Ingredients

1 pear (may also use apples, peaches or nectarines)
1 cup milk
1 tablespoon cornflour or 2 tablespoons sago
1 free range egg (beaten)
1 tablespoon sugar
¼ teaspoon vanilla extract
¼ cup vanilla ice-cream
1 or 2 prunes or dried apricots
1 glace ginger or shaved chocolate (optional)
1 teaspoon sugar
1 pinch mixed spice

COOKS R US

We are an extremely close family and whenever we are together, either celebrating a special occasion or on our regular weekend catch ups, cooking is always a part of it.

Our cooking is inspired by our love of great-tasting, unique and creative meals. Our style is wholesome, low-fat, minimal additive meals with international flair (having lived on three continents). Our meals are suitable for the four generations of our family. We all love cooking because it brings us so much pleasure, laughter, companionship and common goals.

Our family background includes having lived in Malawi, Rhodesia/Zimbabwe and England prior to moving to Perth some 25 years ago. As a family growing up in Africa, we were so lucky to regularly see spectacular wildlife and breathtaking sunsets. Our holiday safaris together are where some of our most treasured family memories came from. We feel truly blessed to all be together. With five grandchildren and their great grandmother, who is over 90 years of age, the years span far and wide in our family, however, we always find a common ground to share love, laughter and the tales of our varied lives over a good meal.

Team Members:
Malcolm Baillie,
Wendy Baillie,
Jack McCormack,
Natalie McCormack

ENTRÉE

FRUIT SOUP
★ Malc's Surprise Soup – you'll never guess

| Preparation Time: 5 mins | Cooking Time: 10 mins | Serves: 2 |

STEP 1 Chop vegetables and fruit into similar sized pieces. Add the stock and curry powder. Bring to the boil then simmer for 7–10 minutes until tender.

STEP 2 Blend the mixture in a food processor until pureed.

STEP 3 Serve with dollop of sour cream and sprinkle with chopped chives.

HINT A family friend from Africa passed this recipe on to us. Really quick, easy and tastes great. It is a fabulous way to get children to eat some fruit and vegetables.

Ingredients
- 1 potato
- 1 piece celery
- 1 onion
- 1 apple
- 1 banana
- 2½ cups chicken stock
- 1 teaspoon curry powder to taste
- sour cream and chives to garnish

MAIN

MOCK T-BONE STEAK
WITH POTATO PANCAKE STACK AND TOMATO CROWN

★ Wendy's T-bone look-a-like

Preparation Time: 20 mins   **Cooking Time:** 35 mins   **Serves:** 4

STEP 1 Cover a grill tray with foil. In a bowl mix steak mince, with soup mix, Worcestershire sauce and tomato sauce. Form four t-bone shapes from the meat mixture. Place strips of bacon around outer edges and fasten in place with tooth pick. Place carrot sticks in centre position for bone. Place on the grill rack.

STEP 2 Mix together all basting mixture ingredients, then baste meat with the mixture on the top side. Place under grill and turn when golden. Baste and grill the other side until golden.

STEP 3 While the t-bones cook, prepare the potato pancake stack. Grate the potatoes, carrots (no need to peel) and brown onion. Finely dice chives or parsley. Lightly beat the egg. Combine all ingredients and mix well.

STEP 4 Add tablespoonfuls of potato mixture into heated, oiled pan and flatten into pancake shape. Cook over low heat for 5 minutes or until crisp, turning once.

STEP 5 Prepare the tomato crown. Cut the top of each tomato around the circumference. Open tomato and sprinkle bread crumbs and cheese on top. Season with salt and pepper. Grill until the tomato is tender and the cheese melted.

STEP 6 Plate up t-bones, potato pancakes and tomatoes and serve with a little sweet chilli sauce.

Ingredients
T-bone steaks
500g steak mince
2 tablespoons mushroom soup mix
2 tablespoons Worcestershire sauce
¼ cup tomato sauce
4 bacon rashers
1 boiled carrot (cut in strips)
salt and pepper

Basting Mixture
2 tablespoons oil
2 tablespoons Worcestershire sauce
2 tablespoons chutney

Potato Pancake Stack
2 large potatoes
1 carrot
1 brown onion
¼ cup chives or parsley
1 egg
¼ cup self raising flour
sweet chilli sauce
vegetable oil

Tomato Crown
4 tomatoes
4 tablespoons grated cheese
4 tablespoons bread crumbs
salt and pepper

DESSERT

LEMON VELVET

★ Jack's Lemon Special

Preparation Time: 5 mins **Cooking Time:** 10 mins to chill **Serves:** 4

STEP 1 Mix all ingredients together and place in serving glasses.

STEP 2 Decorate with raspberries and/or cream on top. Serve with boudoir biscuits or almond macaroons.

HINT Sometimes Wendy puts a chocolate surprise in the middle for the children to seek out and find.

Ingredients

300g bottle lemon butter
300ml whipped cream
400g thick plain yoghurt
icing sugar to taste
raspberries and whipped cream, boudoir biscuits and almond macaroons to serve

INSPIRED BY WINE

The four of us originally met when Shaun and Courtney started playing in a band together, and over the years we have become best friends. We are all crazy about fabulous food and fine wine and would love nothing more than to be dining out every night, however, our budgets don't allow for that! We've substituted fine dining out with fine dining in, and we now spend at least one night a week cooking together.

We have our own vegetable gardens and this inspires our culinary adventures, as does the local organic produce available at the time. We love fresh ingredients! Rather than cook a single dish together, we often produce a feast of different dishes, the most popular theme being seafood, closely followed by Indian and Mexican.

Kestin and I tend to specialise in the main dish, while Shaun is good with starters and Courtney has become known as the dessert expert. All four of us are good with the wine.

Team Members: Courtney Murphy, Jane Murphy, Kestin Owens and Shaun Street

ENTRÉE

HUMMUS BI TAHINA
WITH WARM TURKISH BREAD

★ Hummus Bi Tahina

Preparation Time: 5 mins   **Cooking Time:** 10 mins   **Serves:** 4

STEP 1 Place the chick peas in the food processor along with the garlic, lemon juice, and water. Process for about a minute or until smooth. If too thick, add more water. Stir in the tahina and spices. Taste, and add more lemon juice/tahina/cumin/paprika as appropriate.

STEP 2 Spread the hummus into a shallow bowl, drizzle with olive oil, sprinkle with paprika and garnish with lemon slices and finely chopped parsley. Refrigerate until ready to serve.

STEP 3 Cut Turkish bread into long thin triangles. Warm the Turkish bread in the oven until warmed through and slightly crisp. Serve immediately with the hummus.

Ingredients
2 x 400g cans chick peas (drained and rinsed)
1 loaf Turkish bread
3 cloves garlic (crushed)
1 lemon (juiced)
¼ cup water
3 tablespoons tahina
½ to 1 teaspoon cumin
½ teaspoon paprika
lemon slices and chopped parsley to garnish

46

MAIN

TAGINE COOKED MOROCCAN MEATBALLS
IN A SPICY TOMATO SAUCE SERVED WITH LEMON COUSCOUS

★ Moroccan Meatballs

Preparation Time: 10 mins **Cooking Time:** 30 mins **Serves:** 2

STEP 1 Preheat oven to a medium to high heat. Put ¼ cup of water into tagine and place in oven.

STEP 2 Add all sauce ingredients into a pot on stove top bring to the boil and simmer for 5 minutes. Transfer sauce to the tagine. Mix sauce with water in tagine and place in oven.

STEP 3 Mix all meatball ingredients together in a bowl. Roll into small meatballs. Place meatballs in the tomato sauce in the tagine and cook in the oven for 25 minutes. Remove and stand.

STEP 4 Prepare the lemon couscous. Add the juice of one small lemon to one cup of boiling water. Place the couscous into a bowl. Pour the water mixture over couscous and cover for a few minutes. Stir and serve. Serve meatballs in tagine with couscous.

Ingredients
Sauce
3 cups pureed, super ripe tomatoes
1 teaspoon paprika
1 teaspoon cumin
1 small chilli finely chopped
1 sugar cube
finely chopped parsley and coriander
salt and pepper and dash olive oil

Meatballs
200g beef mince
1 small red onion finely chopped
1 teaspoon paprika
1 teaspoon cumin
parsley and coriander (finely chopped)
1 egg
salt and pepper

Lemon Couscous
1 small lemon juiced
boiling water
2 cups couscous

DESSERT

BANANA FRITTERS IN BUTTERSCOTCH SAUCE

Preparation Time: 10 mins **Cooking Time:** 15 mins **Serves:** 4

STEP 1 Whisk the buttermilk and cinnamon together until combined. Combine the breadcrumbs and coconut in a separate shallow bowl.

STEP 2 Dip a banana into the buttermilk to coat well, then roll in the breadcrumb mixture to coat well. Transfer to a plate or tray. Repeat with remaining bananas. Refrigerate until required.

STEP 3 For the butterscotch sauce, place the cream, sugar, butter and vanilla essence in a medium heavy-based saucepan. Stir over medium heat for 5 minutes or until well combined. Increase heat to high and bring to the boil. Reduce heat to low and simmer, uncovered, stirring often, for 5 minutes or until the sauce thickens slightly. Remove the pan from the heat. Set aside for 2 hours or until cooled to room temperature.

STEP 4 Heat the vegetable oil in a 22cm frying pan over a medium heat. Cook the bananas, turning, for 2–3 minutes until golden. Transfer to a plate lined with paper towel. Serve the fritters with the ice cream squares and butterscotch sauce.

Ingredients
¾ cup buttermilk
large pinch ground cinnamon
⅓ cup multigrain breadcrumbs
⅓ cup McKenzies desiccated coconut
4 ripe lady finger bananas peeled
1 cup vegetable oil
vanilla ice-cream squares to serve

Butterscotch Sauce
⅔ cup thin cream
¾ cup firmly packed brown sugar
2½ tablespoons butter cubed
2 teaspoons vanilla essence

HINT Serve butterscotch sauce at room temperature.

KITCHEN WITCHES

The Kitchen Witches are a magical combination in the kitchen. The team consists of Amanda, Head Witch; Mum also known as nanny; Janet or Sous Witch (not sewerage); Pam, our Witch de Partie (who loves to party) and our favourite teenage witch, Apprentice Witch, Alanna.

What inspires our cooking style is simple, it's whatever we feel like eating at the time or whatever occasion we have coming up. We often like to celebrate our birthdays with different cuisines, and if anyone has seen a new and different recipe, we plan to have a lunch or dinner at the weekend so we can all try it with a couple of glasses of wine! We love cooking together, because we all enjoy cooking and we have a great time doing it. Our styles are different and we are all great at a variety of dishes from canapes to desserts and, most importantly, cocktails to match.

The majority of our family are from England and even though we have been in Australia for 21 years, we still have a soft spot for a traditional cold Christmas. As such we like to celebrate Christmas in July every year. It's just our immediate family here, so we like to think we are the ones creating our own Aussie-British fusion family recipes that can be passed down to future generations.

Team Members: Amanda Southern, Alanna Wyse, Janet Waters, Pam Wyse.

ENTRÉE

ASPARAGUS WRAPPED IN BACON WITH CHEESE SAUCE

★ Nan's Asparagus

Preparation Time: 10 mins   **Cooking Time:** 10 mins   Serves: 4

STEP 1 Begin with the cheese sauce. Melt the butter in a saucepan and add flour, stir together and look for the mixture to change to a white colour. Add the milk, stir briskly to ensure no lumps form in the sauce. Once it has a nice consistency, add mustard powder and cheese and stir through until the cheese is melted. Turn heat down and keep warm.

STEP 2 Blanch asparagus spears in boiling water for 2 minutes, then drain and pat dry.

STEP 3 While the asparagus is blanching, fry bacon rashers. Once cooked, wrap the a bacon rasher around four asparagus spears and pour over cheese sauce.

Ingredients
16 asparagus spears
4 rashers bacon
4 tablespoons butter
4 tablespoons flour
1 teaspoon mustard powder
2 cups milk
2 cups grated cheese

HINT For a twist, try frying prosciutto instead of bacon, for a crispier hit.

MAIN

STUFFED ROAST TURKEY
WITH CRANBERRY JUS, POTATO GRATIN, AND VEGETABLES

★ Turkey McBrie

Preparation Time: 20 mins　　**Cooking Time:** 30 mins　　**Serves:** 4

STEP 1 Cut a slit in the turkey tenderloin, large enough to put brie slices and some stuffing. Set aside.

STEP 2 Combine the stuffing mix with warmed chicken stock. Once mixed, add the sage and macadamia nuts and stir through. Don't over mix; ingredients should be just mixed through. Place the brie slices into turkey and then place the prepared stuffing into the turkey on top of the brie.

STEP 3 Take your stuffed turkey and brown each side in a frying pan. Once browned, place into a hot oven dish and cook in oven for 20 minutes at 180°C, depending on the size of the turkey. Once cooked through, take out and leave to rest.

STEP 4 Mix the sliced potato and onion together in a bowl, pour over the cream and add salt and pepper. Prepare muffin pans by taking greaseproof paper and folding into strips to sit across the bottom of each muffin hole. These strips will become handles to take out the individual gratins. Place the sliced potato and onion into the muffin holes and pour over enough cream to bind. Sprinkle with some grated cheese and place in the oven at 200°C for 15–20 minutes.

STEP 5 Make the cranberry jus by mixing the cranberry sauce with red wine in a saucepan and heat until reduced to nearly half the amount. Turn off heat, then re-warm when time to serve. When warming, stir through a knob of butter, to make the jus nice and glossy.

STEP 6 Take your sliced carrot and cook in boiling water, once cooked, drain and stir through honey and butter.

STEP 7 Blanch broccolini in hot water, take out and drain once cooked. Place stuffed turkey on plate with individual gratin, carrot and broccolini. Sprinkle the turkey with chopped chives. Pour cranberry jus over turkey tenderloin.

Ingredients
4 turkey tenderloins
2 cups stuffing mix
4 tablespoons sage (finely chopped)
8 tablespoons macadamia nuts (finely chopped)
8 tablespoons chicken stock
12 slices brie cheese
4 carrots sliced
4 teaspoons honey
4 teaspoons chives
4 bunchs broccolini
4 potatoes (very finely sliced)
1 onion (very finely sliced)
1 cup cream
12 tablespoons cranberry sauce
8 tablespoons red wine
4 tablespoons butter
salt and pepper

DESSERT

EGGNOG CHEESECAKE
★ Noggy cake

Preparation Time: 8 mins   **Cooking Time:** 5 mins plus 20 mins chilling time   **Serves:** 4

STEP 1 Put the gingernut biscuits in a processor and mix until crumbly. Melt the butter and stir through gingernut crumbs until it comes together like wet sand. Press into the base and sides of a small, spring-form pan and place in the oven for 5 minutes at 180°C. Take out and leave to cool.

STEP 2 Beat together Philadelphia cream cheese and condensed milk. Once smooth, add rum essence and spices and stir through until combined. Pour or spoon into the gingernut shell and place in fridge to set.

STEP 3 To serve, either sprinkle with grated chocolate or a Flake chocolate bar. For a Christmas touch, garnish with a glace cherry and 2 mint leaves.

Ingredients
3 ½ tubs of Philadelphia Cream Cheese
4 tablespoons sweetened condensed milk
4 teaspoons rum essence
2 teaspoons cinnamon
2 teaspoons nutmeg
2 packets gingernut biscuits
2 tablespoons butter

HINT This is one of the quickest and tastiest Christmas desserts around. You can also use rum essence instead of actual rum to make it more child friendly!

THOMAS FAMILY

Nancy was born just north of Toronto, in Ontario, Canada. Her family immigrated to Perth when she was eight years old. She became a primary school teacher and spent all of her spare time with friends on the beach.

She set out backpacking around the world with her sister in 1991. In a train station in Lisbon, Portugal, she met Dean, who was travelling around with a couple of his mates from Melbourne. They both went back to Australia and shared a long distance romance for a few years, eventually marrying and settling in Perth. They now have two fabulous children; Jacob, 12, who enjoys playing basketball and plays the saxophone in the school jazz band, and Chelsea, 10, who is a keen hip-hop dancer, plays the piano and the clarinet.

We spend a lot of time out in our back garden. The BBQ is the main cooking utensil in our house! We use it all year round. We all share a love of fresh seafood and will often cook a variety of courses to sample different kinds. Everyone contributes. The boys will even catch our dinner sometimes! Christmas is often at our house and the whole turkey is done in our BBQ. Many lazy summer days are spent poolside with family and friends. This is our lifestyle and we love it!

Team Members:
Nancy, Jacob,
Chelsea, Dean

ENTRÉE

FRENCH ONION SOUP
★ Bread Boats

Preparation Time: 5 mins   **Cooking Time:** 40 mins   **Serves:** 4

STEP 1 Melt butter in a frying pan and cook onions slowly until golden. Sprinkle with flour and stir for a few minutes to cook. Season with salt and pepper.

STEP 2 Add stock, stirring constantly and bring to boil. Simmer partially covered for 30 minutes. Slice the French stick, cover bread with grated cheese and place under the griller until cheese melts. Place one or two pieces of the French bread stick on top of the soup and serve.

HINT If you tear up chopping onions, wear sunglasses! Also, try to use deep bowls as you want the bread to float.

Ingredients
3 tablespoons butter
3 large onions (thinly sliced)
1 tablespoon flour
½ teaspoon salt
5 cups beef stock
French bread and grated cheese
pepper

MAIN

CHILLI MUSSELS
★ Don't look too closely

| **Preparation Time:** 30 mins | **Cooking Time:** 10 mins | **Serves:** 1 |

STEP 1 Place the mussels in the sink and cover with cold water for about 30 minutes. Remove the little bit of seaweed from the outside of each mussel. If the mussel shell is cracked or the mussel is open discard it.

STEP 2 Put the tomato based pasta sauce in a large pot. Cut the lemons in quarters; squeeze in the juice and then place the lemon in the pot as well. Add tabasco and chilli, to your liking. Add the mussels and cover with a lid. The sauce will come to the boil and very quickly and all the mussels will open up. This means they are cooked. Remove from heat.

STEP 3 Serve over a bed of cooked pasta with some crusty bread to slop up all the yummy sauce.

Ingredients
400g per person fresh local mussels
1 x 750g jar tomato pasta sauce per kg of mussels
½ fresh lemon per serve
tabasco sauce
red chillis
100g spaghetti per serve
crusty sourdough bread & butter

HINT This is our family 'signature dish' which we cook for our rellies visiting from overseas. It is really easy yet impressive. We eat 1kg of mussels when it is just the four of us, so work on 400g per adult.

DESSERT

BUTTER TARTS
★ Nanna's Canadian Butter Tarts

Preparation Time: 10 mins   **Cooking Time:** 15 mins   **Serves:** makes 12 tarts

STEP 1 Mix the sugar, sultanas, egg, butter and vanilla together in a bowl until air bubbles form.

STEP 2 Line a muffin tin with pastry to form pastry cups. Fill with the tart mixture.

STEP 3 Bake at 200°C for 15 minutes or until pastry is cooked. When cool dust with icing sugar to decorate.

HINT We use prepared pastry sheets, however, you can use short crust pastry if you have the time to make your own.

Ingredients
1 cup brown sugar firmly packed
1 cup sultanas
1 egg
1 tablespoon butter
½ teaspoon vanilla
prepared pastry sheets
icing sugar for garnishing

ZUVELA FAMILY

Our family is from the island of Korčula off the Dalmatian coast of Croatia. Nada was born there while Lydia, Tania and Elena were born in Australia. Nada and Lydia's parents and grandparents were also born and lived in Croatia. Elena and Tania's father (Nada's husband) was born in Australia to Croatian parents.

Our cooking is not so much inspired by anything in particular, as it is determined by what's in season throughout the year. We use whatever is fresh and available. The cooking style is essentially Mediterranean and uses a lot of vegetables, fish and olive oil as well as some pasta and rice.

The menu for special family occasions changes depending on whose birthday it is, however we have a regular Sunday dinner at Mum and Dad's place where zelje, a dish made from boiled greens and potatoes, is always on the table. Usually it's served with bread and grilled chops but sometimes it's with fish, goat or squid.

Nada's cooking and style in the kitchen has been a big influence on us, particularly when we were younger. While we've now developed our own dishes based on what we like, Mum's encouragement definitely fostered our understanding and love of food as well as cooking. She's the reason that we all feel confident in what we do in the kitchen, but it can be a drawback when we're all in there at the same time!

Team Members: Elena, Tania, Nada, Lydia

ENTRÉE

MUSSELS COOKED IN WINE

★ Mušule u bjelo vino

Preparation Time: 5 mins **Cooking Time:** 8–10 mins **Serves:** 4

STEP 1 Remove any mussels that are open.

STEP 2 Place all ingredients into a large pot and cover with a tight fitting lid. Cook for 2 minutes on a high heat then check that mussels are starting to open. Stir with a wooden spoon to distribute the wine and herbs then replace lid and cook for another minute, giving the pot a shake to move the mussels around. Continue to cook until most of the mussels have just opened then remove from heat.

STEP 3 Serve straight from the pot or put into deep bowls for individual serves. Use the mussel shells to scoop up the juices.

HINT Take the mussels off the heat as soon as they've just opened to retain their plumpness.

Ingredients

1kg mussels (washed and debearded)
250ml white wine
3 garlic cloves
1 bay leaf
3–4 tomatoes (chopped roughly)
1 onion (sliced into rings)
½ lemon (cut into quarters)
20ml olive oil
2 tablespoons dried oregano
5 tablespoons fresh parsley

MAIN

SQUID INK RISOTTO
★ Crni Risot

Preparation Time: 10 mins　　**Cooking Time:** 20 mins　　**Serves:** 4

STEP 1 Clean the squid by removing the head and tentacles from the body, carefully separating and setting aside the small ink sac. Remove the backbone and cut the body and tentacles into small, even sized pieces.

STEP 2 Heat oil in a large pot then add onion and cook until translucent. Add garlic and cook until fragrant then add the white wine and the pierced ink sac. Cook, stirring continuously, for 2 minutes then add the rice. Cook until most of the liquid has been absorbed by the rice. Add approximately 1 cup of the stock, stirring over high heat until mostly absorbed. Continue adding stock and water (approximately ½ cup at a time), allowing the rice to absorb nearly all the liquid. Taste the rice regularly throughout this process to determine how cooked it is.

STEP 3 When the rice is almost cooked through, add a little more water and the squid pieces then cook for another 3–4 minutes, or until the squid is just cooked. Season with salt and pepper then turn off the heat and allow to rest.

STEP 4 Finely chop the parsley and extra cloves of garlic together and stir into the risotto. Serve sprinkled with extra parsley.

Ingredients
- 1 large squid with ink sac intact
- 1 onion (finely chopped)
- 3–4 tablespoons olive oil
- 2–3 garlic cloves (finely chopped)
- 1½ cups arborio rice
- 200ml white wine
- 500ml fish or vegetable stock (heated)
- 200ml boiling water
- salt and pepper to taste

To Serve
- parsley
- 2 garlic cloves

HINT Fresh or frozen squid can be used for this recipe, although fresh squid are better as the ink is blacker.

DESSERT

PANCAKES
WITH CHOCOLATE AND WALNUTS

★ Palačinke (pala-chin-ké)

Preparation Time: 5 mins **Cooking Time:** 15 mins **Serves:** 6

STEP 1 Beat egg and milk together with salt and vanilla essence until frothy. Add flour and beat until smooth and free of lumps. The mixture should be the consistency of a thin cake batter - add more flour or milk as required.

STEP 2 Heat a shallow frying pan or crepe pan to very hot then add a small amount of butter to coat the pan. Using a soup ladle, add the mixture to the pan and swirl quickly so the batter covers the pan in a thin, even layer. Cook until the top of the pancake is dry and the underside is lightly browned. Flip and cook the other side. Slide onto a flat plate and repeat with the remaining pancake batter. Cover lightly with foil to keep warm.

STEP 3 For the filling, break the chocolate into small, even sized pieces and place over a double boiler or microwave until melted. Add brandy or rum if desired. Spread 1–2 tablespoons of chocolate onto each pancake, sprinkle with walnuts, and then either roll or fold into quarters. Sprinkle with vanilla sugar and serve immediately with cream or ice-cream.

Ingredients
Pancakes
1 egg
1½ cups plain flour
1 teaspoon vanilla essence
500ml milk
pinch salt
butter for cooking
Filling
200g dark chocolate
½ cup walnuts (shelled and finely chopped)
2 tablespoons brandy or rum (optional)
To serve
ice-cream or cream
vanilla sugar

HINT Pancakes can be made ahead of time. Cover with aluminium foil and keep warm until ready to serve with the chocolate filling.

THE QUAFFERS

The Quaffers are captained by self-proclaimed foodie, free-range Phil. The team is made up of Bill Tom (a man so big he needs two names), Tangy Tan and Saucy Sarah. We are long time friends brought together by a passion for cooking, good food and sharing great wine. We love to cook for each other hosting monthly dinner club parties where each tries to 'out cook' the previous host. These parties are always flamboyant and involve plenty of gratuitous mastication.

Our strength is diversity, with each of us possessing individual style and flair. Our inspiration is derived from new season ingredients and chefs like Maggie Beer, Curtis Stone and Peter Evans.

Phil and Bill Tom are mates from university and, in their day, they were renowned for feeding the masses. Meals like a kryovak rump, big enough to feed 20 people (purchased on an unsuspecting parent's butcher's account), and roasted slowly over coals in a 44 gallon drum. After Uni both the boys travelled to Canada where Phil's love of food scored him a job cooking in a restaurant at a ski resort. This in turn kept the housemates happily fed on restaurant 'leftovers'.

The girls, Tanya and Sarah, have been best friends forever and, through mutual friends, we all met up a couple of years ago and our dinner club was born.

Team Members: Bill Tom Howard, Phillip Dikih, Tanya Denman-Murphy, Sarah Moore

ENTRÉE

MUSHROOM AND HALOUMI BRUSCHETTA

★ Miss Moore's Moreish Mushrooms

Preparation Time: 5 mins   **Cooking Time:** 10 mins   **Serves:** 4

STEP 1 Slice the haloumi length ways, about 5mm in thickness. In a frying pan heat a little olive oil over a high heat. Add the haloumi and cook for about 40 seconds each side, looking for a nice golden crisp colour. Set aside. Once cool enough to touch, cut into pieces about the size of a 5 cent piece.

STEP 2 Add a little more olive oil in the frying pan. Add the sliced mushrooms over high heat for 30 seconds, then add the butter. By adding the butter to the mushrooms, rather than the mushrooms to the butter, will avoid the butter burning. Stir occasionally.

STEP 3 Once the button mushrooms are nearly cooked through; add the enoki and the haloumi, cook for 1 minute. Turn off the heat. Stir in the balsamic glaze and parsley and then season to taste. Serve on thickly sliced toasted ciabatta bread and drizzle with olive oil.

Ingredients

250g sliced button mushrooms
80g enoki mushrooms
150g haloumi cheese
¼ cup roughly chopped flat leaf parsley
1 tablespoon butter
1 teaspoon balsamic glaze
olive oil
salt and pepper
1 loaf ciabatta bread

HINT Enoki mushrooms are more expensive but the results are worth it. Any mushrooms will work fine.

FENNEL SEED CRUSTED PORK LOIN
WITH FENNEL AND APPLE PUREE

★ Phil's Free Range Pork & Fennel 3-ways

Preparation Time: 30 mins **Cooking Time:** 25 mins **Serves:** 4

STEP 1 For the pork chops; place all the dry ingredients into a mortar and pestle and grind together. Once the fennel seeds have broken down, mix in the lemon zest. Spread the dry mix onto a plate. Rub the pork chops with a little oil. Place the chops onto the dry mix plate and cover liberally. This makes the lovely crust.

STEP 2 In a frying pan, add oil and heat. Seal both sides of the chops and give them a nice golden colour. Place under a grill on moderate heat. Cook for approximately 20 minutes, turning after 10 minutes.

STEP 3 For the puree; peel, core and roughly chop the apples. Cut the tips off the fennel, halve, take out the core and roughly chop. Put apples and fennel into a pot with stock and water. Cover and bring to the boil. Simmer for 15 minutes or until soft. Drain and blitz with a bamix or blender. Season to taste.

STEP 4 For the coleslaw; finely slice all the salad ingredients. Place sliced ingredients into a mixing bowl with the herbs.

STEP 5 For the dressing; whisk yoghurt, olive oil, caster sugar, and orange juice together. Add a splash of tabasco and season to taste. Mix through.

Ingredients

Pork Chops
4 thick free range pork rib cutlets
3 tablespoons fennel seeds
1 teaspoon white pepper seeds
½ teaspoon rock salt
½ lemon (juiced)

Puree
2 granny smith apples
1 baby fennel bulb
1 cup vegetable stock
1 cup water

Coleslaw
¼ red cabbage
¼ green cabbage
1 red onion
1 fennel bulb
4 radishes
¼ cup roughly chopped, flat leaf parsley, mint and tarragon

Salad dressing
1 small tub natural yoghurt
1 tablespoon olive oil
2 teaspoons caster sugar
1 tablespoon wholegrain mustard
juice from 1 orange
good splash Tabasco
salt and pepper

HINT After the pork chops are cooked, allow the meat to rest on an oven rack so that the crust does not go soggy in the meat juices.

DESSERT

APPLE SPONGE
WITH VANILLA BEAN CUSTARD

★ Big 'Willies' Cake

Preparation Time: 10 mins   **Cooking Time:** 20 mins   **Serves:** 2

STEP 1 For the cake; grease 2 shallow 10cm round cake tins. Preheat oven to 180°C. Place apple, butter, lemon juice, brown sugar, water and cinnamon in frying pan. Cook on high heat for approximately 5 minutes until apples start to go soft. Drain half of the apples and place in cake tins. Leave the remaining apples with their juice to simmer on low heat until mixture thickens and becomes syrupy.

STEP 2 In a bowl mix eggs with an electric beater until fluffy. Add sugar and beat again. Sift flour into egg mixture and mix in. Pour onto apple in cake tins and bake for 20 minutes.

STEP 3 For the custard; whisk egg yolks and sugar together in a heatproof bowl. In a saucepan put the cream, milk and vanilla bean (cut in half lengthways) and bring to boil while stirring. Remove from heat and pour gradually into egg mixture while continually whisking. Transfer the mixture back to the saucepan and cook on low heat while continuously stirring. Custard is cooked when it thickens slightly and coats the back of a spoon.

STEP 4 Serve the sponge upside down with syrupy apples on top surrounded by a pool of custard.

HINT Cream, milk and vanilla bean mixture once boiled will froth up quickly so be careful.

Ingredients

Cake
2 eggs
1/3 cup caster sugar
1/3 cup cornflour
1/4 cup self raising flour
2 green apples (peeled and sliced)
1 tablespoon butter
4 tablespoons brown sugar
1/4 cup water
1/2 teaspoon cinnamon
juice from 1/2 lemon

Custard
3 egg yolks
1/3 cup sugar
150 ml milk
100 ml cream
1/4 vanilla bean (about an inch)

TEAM DA'HUSP

Although our culture is western, our cooking heritage is Chinese. My parents were raised in the Canton region of China. When they migrated to America, they embraced their new culture; democracy, coffee, television, telephones, everything except… the hamburger.

Growing up poor in Chicago did not mean eating poor. Meals were delicious and passionately prepared from fresh ingredients. The aromas, colours and textures emerging from our Chinese kitchen confirmed in my young mind that cooking engaged all five senses. Food was about nourishing the body, feasting the eyes, feeding the heart and inspiring the mind. Eating was the enjoyment of sharing a meal together, celebrating with family and friends.

Birthdays and holidays were special; it was when we were allowed SUGAR!!! It was during the Lunar New Year or at weddings when the best food was served. Menus were planned in advance; ingredients gathered and the preparation took days. Guests talked about banquets for weeks, rating dishes like a competition.

Today, we cook a wide variety of dishes and styles, including recipes from my parents. But as an artist, I can't help tinkering, creating, and evolving food, like my art. We substitute ingredients, cross cultures, and invent processes to suit our tastes and ideas. Would my parents be horrified? Even my mother adds 'ketchup' to her version of BBQ pork. Living in multicultural Melbourne has opened our palettes to a huge range of fresh ingredients, herbs and spices, influencing how we eat and cook.

In our small house, we are never far from the kitchen, where our large pile of recipes reside, gleaned from magazines, newspapers, TV programs, friends, and relatives. The question, What's for tea? is never far from the boys' minds. As I watch them venture into the world, I am thrilled that their passion for food and cooking brings some of the venturing into our kitchen.

Team Members:
Spencer, Huon, David

ENTRÉE

SAN CHOI BOW (LETTUCE CUP) WITH FRIED HALOUMI CHEESE

★ Cheesy Bow

Preparation Time: 5 mins   **Cooking Time:** 5 mins   **Serves:** 4

STEP 1 Cut haloumi into 5mm slices. Oil a frying pan and wait until the oil is hot. Lower the temperature and place the cheese in the pan, moving the slices to prevent them sticking. Flip when golden brown. Place on greaseproof paper to remove excess oil. Reserve for plating.

STEP 2 Thinly slice the purple onion. Sprinkle sea salt and mix thoroughly. Drizzle olive oil over the onion and salt mix and reserve for plating. Wash and dry all the other salad ingredients. Cut cherry tomatoes in half, cut cucumbers into chunks, remove pips from olives and cut olives in half. Place lettuce cups on plates, building the salad inside the cups with all the ingredients, arranging the colours and textures like a Caravaggio painting.

STEP 3 Create the dressing. Chop the lemon grass, garlic, and rosemary finely, or mash together with the salt and pepper in a mortar and pestle. Shake together with olive oil in a jar. Spoon into each lettuce cup and drizzle onto plate around the lettuce.

Ingredients
- 200g haloumi cheese
- 4 cupped leaves iceberg lettuce (size of a rice bowl)
- 20 leaves purple oak leaf or salanova red butter lettuce or equivalent
- 24 green olives
- 1 punnet (250g) cherry tomatoes
- 1 small/medium purple onion
- 2 Lebanese cucumbers
- olive oil
- sea salt

Dressing
- 1/3 cup of olive oil
- 1 clove of garlic
- ½ stick of lemongrass (or lemon juice)
- small sprig of rosemary
- salt and pepper

HINT Haloumi cheese is preserved in salt water. You can soak the cheese overnight or for a couple of days in a container of fresh water to remove some of the saltiness before frying.

MAIN

GRILLED CHAR SIEW
(BBQ PORK) WITH SNOW PEAS, ENOKI MUSHROOMS AND RICE NOODLES

★ Le Char Siew Nouveau

Preparation Time: 30 mins　　**Cooking Time:** 20–25 mins　　**Serves:** 6

STEP 1 Mix marinade ingredients in a bowl. Cut pork loin into 6 pieces of 2cm maximum thickness. Place pork and marinade together, mixing thoroughly, into a sealable plastic bag in the refrigerator. Marinate for 2 hours or overnight.

STEP 2 Place marinated pork onto tray under griller for 20–25 minutes, turning meat over around the 12–14 minute mark, when the edges crisp and the top begins to turn a golden brown. Use some of the remaining marinade sauce for basting. Reserve the remainder of the sauce for the gravy.

STEP 3 Place noodles into pot of cold water, covering thoroughly for 5 minutes. Place a kettleful of boiled water into a heatproof container. Place the snow peas into this water for 2 minutes and stir with chopsticks, remove and plunge them into a container of cold water, stirring until cooled. Top and tail the cooled snowpeas and reserve for plating.

STEP 4 Drain noodles. Pour boiling water over the noodles and bring to boil for a few minutes. Check to suit your level of 'al dente'. Cool with some cold water to prevent further cooking. Drain and reserve for plating.

STEP 5 Mix the sauce. Combine reserve marinade, stock (or water) and approximately 3 teaspoons of cornflour (pre-mixed with a small amount of water) and simmer until thickened. Salt and pepper to taste.

STEP 6 Place drained noodles on plates, with snowpeas and enoki mushrooms (rinsed and separated). Slice rested (4–5 minutes) pork into 1½ to 2 cm strips and arrange on plate. Spoon sauce over meat and around noodles.

Ingredients
1kg boneless pork loin (trimmed)
180g fresh snow peas
100g enoki mushrooms
375g flat white Rick noodles

Marinade
4 teaspoons soy sauce
6 teaspoons sugar
1 teaspoon light soy or teriyaki sauce
1 teaspoon tomato sauce
1 teaspoon oyster sauce
1 teaspoon hoisin sauce

Sauce
Remainder of marinade
1 cup of chicken stock or water
corn flour

HINT Grill pork until edges begin to crisp and the thin layer of fat is rendered and glistening to a light red hue. Then turn over. Let meat rest 4–5 minutes before slicing and plating.

DESSERT

CRISPY APPLE PUFFS
★ Apple Munchies

Preparation Time: 5 mins **Cooking Time:** 15–20 mins **Serves:** Makes 12 pastries

STEP 1 Pre-heat oven on high (220°C for conventional oven, 200°C for fan forced oven). Lightly oil or butter two flat trays. Thaw two sheets of puff pastry. Cut eat sheet into six pieces and arrange on trays.

STEP 2 Peel, core and slice apples into 5mm thick pieces and arrange 4–5 slices on each pastry. Place 4–5 dabs of butter on top of the apples on each pastry. Sprinkle ½ teaspoon of brown sugar over the apples on each pastry.

STEP 3 Place trays in hot oven for 15–20 minutes until golden colour. Cool on rack before lightly dredging with icing sugar.

Ingredients
2 sheets puff pastry
3 apples
6 teaspoons brown sugar
4 teaspoons butter
icing sugar

HINT Be sure to turn the tray around if your oven bakes unevenly.

THE FIGHTING MONGOOSES

Rebecca (Bec) and Fliq met at the tender age of 12, back in grade 7, and formed a friendship that continues to grow through the years. They both found a love of baking off the back of their parent's somewhat lazy approach to cooking baked goods. Bec and Fliq's main cooking influences come from their families, with their earliest cooking memories involving baking with their grandmothers.

Matt and Josh had a chance meeting six years ago, and have been best friends ever since. Catch ups between the two have always involved various delicious foods, and given the diverse dietary requirements of the two, the preparation of food has always been an important part of the cooking process.

When Bec and Matt met and started dating the four of us all became great friends and find ourselves drawn together by our love of cooking. We are passionate about transforming traditional dishes through slight variations catering to our dietary requirements, and also adding a modern twist. We have each shared our old family favourites amongst one another and these still hold a special place within our book of tricks. For example, Fliq's grandparents used to make what is fondly known as 'Jam Rollie Pollie,' whilst Bec's made 'Grandma Cake'. Matt says that his Grandmother and Dad are always battling it out for the title of who does the best traditional English roast.

Team Members:
Matt Aspland,
Rebecca Scorgie,
Fliq Holloway,
Josh Fergeus

ENTRÉE

EGGPLANT CRISPS
WITH HERB AND GARLIC DRESSING

★ Josh's Eggplant Kajiggers

Preparation Time: 20 mins **Cooking Time:** 10 mins **Serves:** 2

STEP 1 Cut eggplant into thin slices. Salt and allow to sit for 15 minutes.

STEP 2 Mix all dressing ingredients together until well combined. Add salt or pepper to taste.

STEP 3 Heat oil in a shallow frying pan. Rinse eggplant in cold water and pat dry with paper towel.

STEP 4 Cook eggplant until golden brown on each side then place on paper towel to absorb excess oil. Serve drizzled with dressing.

HINT To make them look a bit fancier place on top of a bed of rocket.

Ingredients

Crisps
1 eggplant
salt
olive oil

Dressing
½ cup olive oil
2 teaspoons minced garlic
1 teaspoon minced chilli
½ cup chopped parsley
½ cup chopped chives
1 lime (juiced)

MAIN

GLUTEN FREE LINGUINE
WITH MIXED VEGETABLES

★ Bec & Matt's Vegetable Pasta

Preparation Time: 20 mins **Cooking Time:** 10 mins **Serves:** 2

STEP 1 Fill a large pot with water, add a pinch of salt then bring to the boil. Add the linguine and cook as per the packet instructions (usually 8–10 minutes).

STEP 2 Heat oil in a frying pan and add the onion, capsicum, zucchini, garlic, chilli and parsley. Cook until just starting to soften.

STEP 3 Add capers, olives and tomatoes and cook for a further 1 minute.

STEP 4 Add the baby spinach and cook until leaves are wilted. Serve on top of the linguine.

HINT If you are not a vegetarian, try adding some bacon and anchovies. As you can tell we like it salty!

Ingredients
250g gluten free linguine
1 capsicum sliced
1 zucchini sliced
1 onion sliced
100g baby spinach
1 cup sliced baby roma tomatoes
¼ cup sliced kalamata olives
3 teaspoons capers
3 teaspoons minced garlic
2 teaspoons minced chilli
chopped parsley to taste
salt
olive oil

DESSERT

GLUTEN FREE BUTTERMILK PANCAKES
WITH ICE-CREAM AND A WILD BERRY AND CHAMBORD SAUCE

★ Miss Fliq's Romantic Berry Pancakes

Preparation Time: 15 mins   **Cooking Time:** 15 mins   **Serves:** 2

STEP 1 Whisk buttermilk and eggs together in large bowl.

STEP 2 Sift flour and sugar into wet ingredients, whisk to combine.

STEP 3 Heat a non stick frying pan to a moderate temperature. Melt a small amount of butter in the pan to grease. Ladle pancake batter into pan, cook for approximately 2 minutes per side till golden brown.

STEP 4 To make berry sauce; place berries, lime juice and sugar into a small saucepan and heat until slightly reduced (stirring occasionally). Make sure not to squash the berries when stirring the sauce as you do not want them to lose shape.

STEP 5 Add chambord to the berry mixture to taste. Plate pancakes, top with ice-cream and pour berry sauce over the stack.

Ingredients

Pancakes
2 cups of buttermilk
2 eggs
¾ cup gluten free self raising flour
¼ cup caster sugar

Berry sauce
350g mixed berries (frozen is okay if out of season)
¼ cup caster sugar
1 lime (juiced)
healthy splash of chambord liqueur

HINT Wait 5 minutes for the ice-cream and berries to melt into a scrumptious pink goo. Perfect for romantic evenings.

THE HAPPY CAFÉ

It was love at first vintage dress sighting when 'The Happy Café' family met through mutual friends. Although we were all born in Australia, you may be forgiven for mistaking us as 'Frenchies'. We all prefer to eat dessert over a main meal any day, and we use baking/cooking as an excuse to sneak a few spoonfuls of raw cake mix! Our philosophy is; any baking catastrophe can be redeemed with dusted icing sugar. We share an inappropriate passion for samples and pies, and enjoy throwing themed tea parties, believing this to be the best way to bring all our friends together.

Our cooking is inspired by our taste buds and flavours that are unusual when combined together. We will try any recipe once and when standing in line at the checkouts, will skim through all the magazines to find the best one. We also find that our travels have allowed us to pick up new recipes from around the world.

Camille developed her love of presenting food from her artistic mother who would often arrange dinner in the shape of faces and nature scenes! In Bec's family, the mantra was either, "It's fend for yourself night," or, "If you don't have dinner, you can just make up for it with a big café lunch the next day!"

A few months ago we made a John Lennon themed cake for a friend's birthday, however, instead of giving it to her we decided to take turns face planting the cake and eating it without hands! (Thus fulfilling a life long fantasy).

One final tip: if you eat off someone else's plate the calories don't count.

Team Members include: Rebekah Pretty, Felicity Hernandez, Sarah White, Camille Hayton.

ENTRÉE

OYSTER MUSHROOM ASPARAGUS SALAD

★ Soldiers and Shrooms Salad

Preparation Time: 10 mins **Cooking Time:** 5 mins **Serves:** 4

STEP 1 Put all the dressing ingredients in a jar and shake, shake, shake.

STEP 2 Cook mushrooms and asparagus on an oiled griddle pan until brown and just tender.

STEP 3 Toast the pine nuts briefly on the grill. (Be careful they burn quickly!).

STEP 4 Prepare the dressing by mixing all of the ingredients together in a bowl. (Except the parsley).

STEP 5 Toss vegetables in a large bowl with parsley and dressing. Arrange in a pretty pyramid on a plate, drizzle with extra dressing, the pine nuts and more fresh parsley.

HINT You can decorate this dish with actual mini toy soldiers! The dish works well because you can adapt it in order to use up ingredients from your fridge, for example, instead of the asparagus you could use beans or snow peas, while the fancy oyster mushrooms could be substituted with regular sliced button mushrooms (although this won't impress your guests as much!).

Ingredients
300g oyster mushrooms
8 asparagus spears (trimmed)
½ cup fresh parsley leaves (finely chopped)
1 tablespoon toasted pine nuts

Dressing
1 teaspoon finely grated lemon rind
1 tablespoon lemon juice
2 tablespoons olive oil
1 clove garlic (crushed)
1 teaspoon chopped parsley

FIG, FENNEL AND BUTTERNUT PUMPKIN LAMB

★ Squashed Figgy Fennel Lamb

Preparation Time: 15 mins   **Cooking Time:** 10 mins   **Serves:** 2

STEP 1 Sprinkle lamb with salt and pepper. Rub rosemary onto each side.

STEP 2 Combine the fennel, salt, pepper, vinegar and sugar in a bowl.

STEP 3 Heat a little oil in a frying pan and grill the figs, pumpkin and fennel until they are caramelised.

STEP 4 In a separate frying pan, sear the lamb for 4 minutes on each side.

STEP 5 To serve, place the fennel mixture on a plate, top with lamb, figs and pumpkin.

HINT Dried figs can be used if figs aren't in season, but ideally for colour and flavour, fresh is best! You could serve the fennel salad raw as a fresher alternative; the aniseed flavour of the fennel is just more intense if it hasn't been grilled. If you love liquorice this is a good thing!

Ingredients
4 lamb cutlets
4 baby fennel bulbs (sliced)
6 figs (halved)
2 cups butternut pumpkin (cubed)
2 tablespoons olive oil
2 teaspoons chopped rosemary
¼ cup white wine vinegar
4 tablespoons brown sugar
salt and pepper to taste

DESSERT

CHOCOLATE FONDUE
WITH BAILEY'S CREAM, HONEYCOMB AND STRAWBERRIES

★ Charlie's heavenly chocolate fondue fountain

Preparation Time: 20 mins **Cooking Time:** None! **Serves:** 4

STEP 1 Whip the cream with an electric beater until soft peaks form. Stir in the Baileys. Stir in more Baileys!

STEP 2 Break chocolate up into pieces and melt in the microwave. Pour the chocolate goodness into a large serving bowl.

STEP 3 Arrange the fruit and honeycomb on a plate (if you haven't already eaten them all), along with the cream and chocolate.

STEP 4 Dip treats or just your fingers into the heavenly river of chocolate!

Ingredients
2 cups cooking chocolate
1 cup of cream
3 tablespoons Baileys Irish Cream
1 bag honeycomb pieces
1 punnet of strawberries

HINT Nothing beats a cascading river of chocolate (cue image of the chocolate waterfall from Charlie and The Chocolate Factory!) as the centerpiece at your dinner party. People will literally flock around it like bees to honey. When you run out of things to dip, just use a shot glass and have shots of pure chocolate heavenly goodness.

76

KAY FAMILY

We are an Aussie-Asian couple who first met in 2005. At the time my cooking skills were somewhat rusty. As our relationship blossomed it was evident that Matt's taste buds were sharp and required nurturing, so I set my sites on refining my skills and cooking my way to his heart via his stomach. My husband and the whole Kay clan just loves good food.

Our nephew, Trent Kay, would visit us weekly and spend a day or two at a time at our place. During these visits he made himself at home in our kitchen and just loved cooking for us, he's a real character. Our niece, Emma Kay Pearce, on the other hand loves food out of the necessity to feed the energy she has. She is a nursing student who has a great passion for sports. She is currently playing in the Australian Hockey team. She is the fittest of the family and is as bubbly as a cup cake in an oven.

I now have a wide variety of cooking styles from Asian to American, Oriental to a little bit of Italian. I guess my inspiration for cooking comes originally from my husband Matt's taste buds, he has a very good palate for what's good. The Kays originally came from Liverpool in the UK on the *Mountaineer* sailboat in 1832. Robert Kay accidentally missed the boat and travelled on the *Lavinia* arriving one month later. The eldest son George was born on the voyage to Australia and the rest is history.

Team Members: Trent Kay, Emma Kay Pearce, Row Kay, Matt Kay

ENTRÉE

BATTERED PRAWNS

★ Tipsy Prawns

Preparation Time: 5 mins   **Cooking Time:** 7 mins   **Serves:** 4

STEP 1 Shell prawns and leave the tails on.

STEP 2 Put flour in a medium bowl, add egg, water, salt, carbonated water, cracked pepper, parsley and mix until all ingredients combined. Place all the shelled prawns in the bowl.

STEP 3 Heat oil in a large deep saucepan. Holding prawns by the tail place them into the saucepan. Deep-fry the prawns until batter is lightly browned and prawns have turned pink. Do not overcrowd the prawns in the saucepan or they will stick together.

STEP 4 Cut lemon in round slices. Place the cooked prawns in the middle of a serving platter and place cut lemon around the outside. Mix the parsley and garlic for dipping. Sprinkle lemon on top to taste.

HINT Make sure the oil is very hot then turn stove to low heat before placing in the prawns, then turn back to medium heat once the prawns are in the pan to avoid splatter.

Ingredients
500g fresh uncooked medium prawns
1½ cups plain flour
½ cup water
¼ cup carbonated water
1 egg
1 teaspoon parsley flakes
1 teaspoon cracked pepper
1 lemon for garnishing
pinch salt
finely chopped parsley for dipping
crushed garlic for dipping
cooking oil, for deep-frying

MAIN

CREAMY CHICKEN PASTA WITH MIXED VEGGIES

★ Matrow's Chicken Special

Preparation Time: 7 mins **Cooking Time:** 15 mins **Serves:** 4

STEP 1 Cook pasta until al dente. While cooking prepare the cheese and white sauce mixes.

STEP 2 Heat oil in a large wok over medium heat. Fry ginger and garlic until slightly brown then add the chicken, mild curry powder, parsley flakes, cracked pepper and fry until brown.

STEP 3 Stirring add the chicken stock, coconut cream. Bring to a simmer then add all the vegetables, cheese sauce and white sauce. Add a little oyster sauce according to taste and simmer.

STEP 4 Put pasta on a serving plate then pour the creamy chicken and vegetables on top to serve.

HINT Serve vegetables 'al dente'.

Ingredients
250g pasta
500g chicken thigh fillets (cut into strips)
2 cubes chicken stock
35g cheese sauce mix
35g white sauce mix
1 broccoli
410g can young corn
425g champignons
165g coconut cream
1 green capsicum (seeded and cut into strips)
1 medium onion (cut into 8 pieces)
1 teaspoon mild curry powder
1 teaspoon oyster sauce
1 teaspoon parsley flakes
1 teaspoon cracked pepper
pinch rock salt
small piece ginger (cut thinly)

DESSERT

PANCAKE DELIGHT
★ Sparky's delight

| Preparation Time: 5 mins | Cooking Time: 5 mins | Serves: 4 |

STEP 1 Place pancake mix in a bowl , add 2 cups of milk and mix until all ingredients are combined.

STEP 2 Place a spoonful of margarine into a large frying pan, then pour batter into the pan and cook until small bubbles appear before turning over and cooking on the other side.

STEP 3 Place pancake on a serving plate, spread with jam and place cut strawberries on one side and sprinkle with icing sugar. Fold over. Sprinkle with icing sugar and drizzle with honey. Serve with a scoop of chocolate ice-cream.

HINT Do not overcook the pancakes, keep them light and fluffy.

Ingredients
300g pancake and pikelet mix
2 cups milk
1 egg extra large
1 cup icing sugar for garnishing
50g margarine for frying
1 punnet strawberry
jam any flavor
honey
chocolate ice cream

TEAM ADOS

Our parents migrated from Greece in the late 1950s and brought with them the tastes and cooking techniques of their own upbringing.

They passed on that richness of culture, heritage, family and hospitality to all three of their children. We in turn have each developed our own cooking skills. Peggy, the eldest, has broadened her skills to many different cuisines including Asian and Italian. Kelly has developed an excellent grasp of both traditional and contemporary cuisines and loves to cook Christmas lunch and dinner every year. Hari, the youngest, has developed great camp cooking skills and has cooked everything from damper and scones to kangaroo and goat in the camp oven.

While we have all developed our own styles and flair, we still love nothing more than coming home to Mum and Dad's. Their home is always filled with great aromas, warm feelings and hearty soul. Fellowship, comfort and love are all essential ingredients for great food.

Kelly's 2 year old son, Alexandros, is the inspiration for our team name 'Ados'. Whenever we ask him what his name is, he says 'Ados' - Alexandros is a bit of a mouthful for a 2 year old, no matter how, extraordinary we think he is.

Team Members: Terpsichori Maragos, Kelly Maragos, Alexandros Marangidis, Paghona Peggy Kerdo, Hari Maragos (at back)

ENTRÉE

CHARGRILLED & SAUTÉED MEDITERRANEAN VEGIES

★ Hari's Mediterranean Vegies

| Preparation Time: 5 mins | Cooking Time: 10 mins | Serves: 4 |

STEP 1 Chargrill the eggplant and zucchini on a griddle plate or under the griller. Take care not to burn – we just need some colour. Set aside and allow to rest for 1-2 minutes.

STEP 2 Add some olive oil to a deep frying pan (preferably one with a lid). Heat the oil over a hot flame. Add the garlic, salt and cracked pepper. Stir and allow oil to be infused by the flavours.

STEP 3 Add the eggplant and zucchini. As they will already have some colour, simply allow them to soften and the flavours of the oil, garlic, salt and pepper to cover and infuse into them. Cover with a lid and let the juices steam and aid in the cooking process.

STEP 4 Add the peppers and mushrooms and toss to mix all ingredients together. Add the oregano and a good splash of balsamic vinegar and cover with a lid. Allow the steam to cook the mushrooms until they are soft, but slightly firm on the inside - almost like 'al dente' pasta.

STEP 5 When done, using a pair of tongs, serve onto a white plate and pour over pan juices. Garnish with fresh parsley, a couple of slices of crusty bread and lemon.

STEP 6 Share with loved ones and enjoy.

Ingredients
- 2 good handfuls button mushrooms (these can either be sliced of served whole)
- 1 eggplant (firm and thinly sliced)
- 1 zucchini (thinly sliced)
- 1 red and 1 yellow capsicum (roasted, peeled, deseeded and sliced)
- 1 teaspoon crushed garlic
- 1 tablespoon good quality extra virgin olive oil
- 1 teaspoon Modena balsamic vinegar
- dried oregano (flakes)
- salt & cracked pepper to taste

HINT Great served with fresh homemade bread, melitzanosalata (eggplant dip) and tzatziki. Also it is great served on a balmy evening with a few glasses of wine. (Dad's of course!).

MAIN

LAMB SOUZOUKAKIA
★ Souzoukakia

| Preparation Time: 20 mins | Cooking Time: 20 mins | Serves: 4 |

STEP 1 In a bowl, place the lamb mince, egg, grated onion, garlic, cumin, parsley, and salt and pepper.

STEP 2 Wet the bread briefly with water. Squeeze the water out with your hands and then add it to the bowl with the lamb mixture.

STEP 3 Knead the mixture until all ingredients are combined. Shape firmly with your hands into small oval meatballs (that look like Aussie Rules footballs).

STEP 4 Heat enough olive oil to shallowly cover a frying pan. Quickly brown the meatballs. When they are all browned, add the ingredients for the tomato sauce. Bring to the boil, then drop the heat and simmer for 20 minutes.

STEP 5 Serve with crumbled feta, good crusty bread and a fresh salad.

HINT The main difference between standard rissoles and 'souzoukakia' is the cumin. This spice – popular in many Mediterranean and Middle Eastern dishes – adds extra levels of both warmth and depth to the souzoukakia allowing the eater to feel nurtured.

Ingredients
Souzoukakia
500g lamb mince
2 slices bread
1 egg
1 tablespoon ground cumin
1 clove garlic (crushed and finely chopped)
1 onion (grated)
fresh parsley
salt
pepper
extra virgin olive oil for frying
Tomato sauce
1 tinned peeled chopped tomatoes
2 cups tomato passata
1 teaspoon chopped chilli
pinch sugar
salt
pepper
To finish
good quality feta (Greek or Bulgarian)
crusty bread

DESSERT

LOUKOUMADES
WITH HONEY AND CHOCOLATE SAUCE
★ Mum's Loukoumades

Preparation Time: 1 hour   **Cooking Time:** 15 mins   **Serves:** 4

STEP 1 Prepare the loukoumades by adding the ingredients together (as if making bread) and placing the dough/mixture near a heat source (an electric blanket has been used many times) and wait until the mixture rises – about an hour.

STEP 2 In a deep pot, heat the oil. Place a little bit of dough into the oil – if it starts to 'fry', the oil is ready. Reduce the heat a little so oil doesn't 'boil', however, remains hot enough to fry with. Get ready to use both hands and a spoon dipped in hot water. Using one hand, grab a handful of the mixture, gently massage and squeeze ball through the fist (between thumb and forefinger). Using the spoon 'cut' ball from fist and place into oil.

STEP 3 Using tongs or a strainer, gently roll the dough over so that all sides are fried. When the balls start to float, allow them to become golden (not brown) and remove from the pan.

STEP 4 When ready, remove from the pot straining as much excess oil as possible. Place on absorbent paper to allow any excess oil to drain off.

STEP 5 Prepare the honey sauce. Pour the honey into a saucepan and heat until honey becomes very runny. Allow to simmer.

STEP 6 Prepare the chocolate sauce. Combine chocolate and cream in a saucepan over low heat and stir until smooth. Allow sauce to stand for 5 minutes.

STEP 7 Once the loukoumades are 'dry', serve with the honey and/or chocolate sauce. Sprinkle a little cinnamon over them and enjoy with good coffee and a little Metaxa brandy.

Ingredients
1 cup plain flour
1 teaspoon yeast
water (enough to make dough consistency)
light olive oil to fry
Honey Sauce
1 tablespoon good quality honey
Chocolate Sauce
125g good quality dark chocolate
¾ cup light cream

HINT Almost taking on the same 'genre' as scones and sponge cake, these are an absolute family favourite.

FOOD FREAKS

The Food Freaks are an avid bunch of foodies. Our lust for preparing food is inspired by our parents. Our parents, John and June, travelled the world before immigrating to South Australia from England with five girls. Lorraine, the eldest child and Linda the second eldest, followed by Jackie, Lisa and Debbie. In 1973, Vicky was born – that made six. Both of our parents loved to cook for the family. As children, we were lucky to experience a vast variety of homemade foods.

We didn't have a great deal of money, however, our parents would make a point of taking us to *George's Seafood Restaurant* in the city whenever possible. Our parents loved to cook so much they took over a restaurant in Gawler in the late 1970's. Dad would cook savoury meals and Mum would cook a beautiful array of cakes and sweets to perfection. We rarely ate any type of take away. Emma is Linda's daughter and is the eldest grandchild. She has subsequently been followed by Matthew, Alex, Elisha, Nikki, Carly, Trista, Eden, Jack, Tayla, Bailey and James.

With six children, our parents often found themselves cooking for several others – friends and friends of friends. Many would turn up just for a tasty meal. Our parents have now both passed away, however, all six children still live close to one another. We love getting together to have family meals with all six children, their partners and their children. Food still brings our family, friends and even friends of friends, together!

We love to recreate Mum and Dad's fabulous dishes as well as creating our own. We feel very lucky to have experienced such a vast range of foods from so many cultures.

Team Members: Victoria Gorst, Emma Skondras, Linda Young, Lorraine Willcourt

ENTRÉE

EGGPLANT BRUSCHETTA
★ Greek Aussie Doorstop

| Preparation Time: 20 mins | Cooking Time: 5 mins | Serves: 4 |

STEP 1 Slice eggplant and sprinkle with salt. Leave for 20 minutes.

STEP 2 Lightly toast bread on both sides. Drizzle one side of the toasted bread with a little olive oil and a light spread of garlic.

STEP 3 Lightly fry haloumi cheese in dry frying pan until golden. Fry the eggplant in a little olive oil on both sides until golden.

STEP 4 Lay the haloumi on top of the bread, followed by the eggplant and sliced tomatoes. Grill until warmed through. Add basil and left over garlic to the olive oil and drizzle over.

Ingredients
4 slices European loaf
1 eggplant
2 tomatoes
4 large slices haloumi cheese (cut 1cm thick)
2 tablespoons fresh garlic
4 tablespoons fresh basil
1/8 cup olive oil

HINT Try using zucchini instead of eggplant to shorten the preparation time.

MAIN

SALMON
WITH ASIAN GREENS ON A BED OF CHIVE MASH

★ Salmon Smash

Preparation Time: 10 mins   **Cooking Time:** 20 mins   **Serves:** 4

STEP 1 Pre-heat the oven to 180°C. Let the fish marinate in a little olive oil, soy sauce and a little of the lemongrass.

STEP 2 Peel, chop and boil the potatoes in a saucepan until soft enough for mashing. Take apart the bok choy, slice the capsicum, and finely dice the red onion.

STEP 3 Bake fish in oven on baking tray for 10 minutes and then pan fry for 1 minute on each side.

STEP 4 Add garlic, ginger, chilli and lemongrass, onto a heated wok with some olive oil. Add the bok choy, red onion, broccoli, capsicum and snow peas to the wok and fry together with the herbs. Add soy sauce and cook for a further 2 minutes. Toast the sesame seeds on separate heated frying pan until golden. Add sesame seeds to the stir-fried vegetables.

STEP 5 Mash potatoes with butter and chives (add milk if you like). Add mash to each plate and top with salmon. Layer with vegetables and drizzle remaining sauce over the whole dish.

Ingredients
- 4 salmon steaks
- 4 bunches baby bok choy
- 1 cup snow peas
- 1 red capsicum (sliced)
- 1 cup broccoli
- 1 red onion
- 5 potatoes
- 2 tablespoons garlic
- 1 tablespoon chilli
- 1 tablespoon ginger
- ½ teaspoon lemongrass
- 1 teaspoon chives
- ¼ cup soy sauce
- 5 tablespoons sesame seeds
- 2 tablespoons butter
- olive oil

HINT The fish and the vegetables can be changed to whatever you like. This is a quick, healthy and delicious meal that anyone can make.

DESSERT

SOFT CHOCOLATE PUDDINGS

★ Gooey Choc Pudding with Cream

Preparation Time: 5 mins   **Cooking Time:** 20 mins   **Serves:** 4

STEP 1 Melt chocolate in a bowl placed over hot water.

STEP 2 Whisk the eggs and flour and then combine with the melted chocolate.

STEP 3 Divide mixture between four greased patty cake pans and cook for 20 minutes, or until the outside is cooked but the centre is soft and gooey.

STEP 4 Serve with whipped cream, chocolate flakes and strawberries or glace cherries.

HINT For an extra gooey caramel centre, try putting a piece of caramel chocolate in the centre of the pudding before baking. This tastes fantastic with white chocolate. Try making an easy chocolate sauce by melting 150g chocolate with 100ml cream over a low heat – pour over cooked pudding and serve with whipped cream.

Ingredients
220g dark chocolate (chopped)
¼ cup flour
3 eggs
1 cup cream
chocolate flakes
strawberries or glace cherries

88

CHIAPPIN FAMILY

Our team is made up of three generations of Chiappin's. We pride ourselves on our diversity and love celebrating the different cultures that make up our family and exploring different ways to share food.

Tony Chiappin, aged 75, is father of Josie, Anthony and Paul, and Nonno to four grandchildren. Tony arrived in Australia from the Veneto region of Italy 58 years ago, bringing with him many traditions relating to the making and preparation of food. Tony loves making salami and sausages, tomato sauce and wine. He married Judith, whose family is from country South Australia; farmers and bakers of English/Irish and German descent.

Josie Revesz, married into a Hungarian family, and has four children, all of whom are actively involved in carrying on the family 'food' traditions. Paul Chiappin, married into a Greek family, avidly developing his skills in the art of the Greek barbeque. Isabella, 14, daughter of Josie, loves to be involved in anything relating to food preparation, and would like to pursue a career in the food industry.

Our family now encompasses the four corners of the world. We even have an Indian uncle, so we have also grown up learning many of his family recipes. Most importantly, we love to be together to celebrate our diversity and share and enjoy the food that we have lovingly prepared.

Team Members: Tony Chiappin, Josie Revesz, Paul Chiappin, Isabella Revesz.

ENTRÉE

OYSTER SHOT AND SMOKED SALMON BRUSCHETTA

★ Paul's Seafood Sensation

Preparation Time: 10 mins   **Cooking Time:** No cooking required   **Serves:** 1

STEP 1 To prepare the smoked salmon bruschetta, slice panini or ciabatta bread thinly, brush with olive oil and toast under the griller.

STEP 2 Spread with cream cheese, and decorate/top with a slice of smoked salmon, thin slices of red onion and capers.

STEP 3 Place one oyster in a shot glass, pour tomato juice over the oyster to just cover it, add a good slurp (1 tablespoon) of vodka and a dab of hot chilli paste.

STEP 4 Present the shot and salmon bruschetta on a plate. They look stunning when placed together you don't need any extra garnishing. Drink the shot, eat the bread and enjoy!

HINT We have come up with many combinations for the oyster shots. The one featured here is the Bloody Mary shot, however, we have also had a combination of wasabi, pickled ginger and sake, lime juice and gin. Use your imagination like we do.

Ingredients
- 2 slices panini or ciabatta bread
- 1 teaspoon olive oil
- 2 teaspoons philadelphia cream cheese
- 2 slices smoked salmon
- 1 teaspoon capers
- 1 oyster
- ½ shot glass of tomato juice
- 1 tablespoon vodka
- dab of hot chilli paste
- 1 red onion as garnish (sliced)

MAIN

PAN FRIED SCOTCH FILLET
SERVED ON A BED OF MUSHROOM & FENNEL RISOTTO WITH RED WINE JUS

★ Fillet Chiappin

Preparation Time: 20 mins **Cooking Time:** 30 mins **Serves:** 6

STEP 1 Pour a few tablespoons of olive oil into a heated frying pan and place the scotch fillets in. Sprinkle with a pinch of sea salt and cracked pepper and brown on each side. Remove from the pan and place onto a baking dish. Allow this to rest in a warm oven for 10 minutes.

STEP 2 While meat is resting, add minced garlic to the pan; allow to sauté a little before adding the red wine. Reduce to a thick sauce.

STEP 3 Heat olive oil and butter in a frying pan until melted. Add onion and garlic and sauté until transparent. Add sliced mushrooms, fennel and porcini mushrooms and sauté until soft. At this point, add the rice and fry with vegetables until it takes on a slightly golden colour.

STEP 4 Heat the stock in a separate saucepan and begin to add to the rice mixture approximately 1 cup at a time until the rice absorbs it, stirring gently the whole time. Add a little salt and cracked pepper to taste. (You can adjust the seasoning at the end of the cooking time.) Keep adding the stock until the rice is 'al dente', and remove from the heat. Cover and allow to stand for a few minutes before adding the parmesan cheese. Stir this through and serve immediately.

STEP 5 To serve, place a cup of risotto in the centre of the plate and then position the scotch fillet on top of the rice. Drizzle the jus over the meat and around the edge of the plate. Serve with steamed green vegetables.

HINT This is a very quick, easy and delicious way to prepare meat. You also have the beginnings of a great jus. We always add a slurp of our homemade red wine, garlic, cracked pepper and salt to the pan juices and let it reduce over heat. Presto – a delicious red wine jus!

Ingredients
6 scotch fillets
3 tablespoons olive oil
2 cloves crushed garlic
1 cup red wine
sea salt and cracked pepper

Risotto
1 tablespoon butter
2 tablespoons olive oil
2 litres of beef stock
3 cups arborio rice
1 brown onion (diced)
1 clove garlic (chopped)
2 large Swiss brown mushrooms (sliced)
10g dried porcini mushrooms, soaked in boiling water
½ bulb of fennel (sliced thinly)
½ cup grated parmesan
sea salt and cracked pepper

DESSERT

CHOCOLATE SELF SAUCING PUDDING

★ Isabella's masterpiece

Preparation Time: 10 mins   **Cooking Time:** 15–20 mins for small serves or 40–45 mins for large serve   **Serves:** 4

STEP 1 Preheat oven to 180°C and butter a 750ml pie dish.

STEP 2 Sift flour, salt, caster sugar, baking powder and cocoa into a bowl. Combine milk, melted butter, egg and vanilla and mix into dry ingredients. Pour into the pie dish.

STEP 3 To make the topping; mix brown sugar and cocoa and sprinkle over pudding batter. Pour boiling water carefully over all ingredients.

STEP 4 Bake for 40–45 minutes until puffed up in the centre and the pudding feels firm when pressed lightly with your fingertips. To serve, spoon out the cake and sauce while hot and dust with icing sugar.

HINT You can make individual puddings by dividing the mixture and topping evenly between four small pie dishes or ramekins (1 cup capacity). These are also lovely served with macerated or fresh raspberries and fresh cream.

Ingredients
125g plain flour
60g caster sugar
1 egg
½ cup milk
40g butter (melted)
2 teaspoons baking powder
pinch of salt
few drops of vanilla

Topping
180g brown sugar
2 tablespoons Dutch cocoa
1 cup boiling water
fresh raspberries and fresh cream to serve

FECHNER FAMILY

We are the Fechner family. We have been getting together for great meals and great wine for over 30 years. Being in the Barossa, food is an important part of our culture and we are never short of a good drop of wine to accompany each dish!

We are sixth generation German descendants still living on our original settlements in the Barossa valley. Between us we have 11 children, which means a lot of baptisms, confirmations, anniversaries, birthdays and get-togethers. So a lot of great food and fine wine is needed to satisfy the hordes, along with the need for creativity to tantalise the vast array of tastebuds. The accolades we receive after a feeding frenzy is all the reward that is needed to compensate for the effort put in.

Dana's father grew up in the depression living mainly on rabbits and galahs. He loved the tender bird meat – his recipe for cooking galah is to put a rock in the oven with the galah and when the rock is soft, throw out the galah and eat the rock! Seriously though, times were tough and we couldn't afford to waste anything. Whatever the animal, it was all eaten, from tongue to toe. Our tastebuds were introduced at a young age to a myriad of exciting, exotic dishes.

Michael's speciality is seafood which came about by being constantly disappointed with fish meals in restaurants over the years. We love all kinds of food, from lamb or pig on a spit to the simple backyard barbecue. It's the season that dictates what we cook and how.

Team Members: Claudia, Huon, Dana, Michael, Clayton

ENTRÉE

PAN-FRIED HALOUMI
WITH SOUR DOUGH CRISPS & RADICCHIO AND WITLOF SALAD

★ Huon's Haloumi

Preparation Time: 15 mins   **Cooking Time:** 15 mins   **Serves:** 1

STEP 1 Slice the sour dough into thin strips, 5mm thick and add a sprinkle of salt and olive oil. Bake in oven at 160°C for 15 minutes or until crispy.

STEP 2 Finely slice the side of the pear and place all salad leaves and pear slices into a bowl. Mix the salad.

STEP 3 Heat a frying pan and add the haloumi and cook for approximately 15 seconds on each side, until it is lightly brown. Serve up on a large plate with the bread and salad dressed with hazelnut oil.

HINT Use vegetable oil as olive oil burns and make sure pan is extremely hot.

Ingredients
2 slices haloumi cheese (5mm thick x 100mm x 50mm)
1/3 bosc pear
3–4 radicchio leaves
3–4 water cress leaves
3–4 mustard cress leaves
4–5 leaves witlof
vegetable oil (for cooking haloumi)
hazelnut oil (salad dressing)
sour dough bread

MAIN

TANGY SAUCED GRILLED FISH

★ Wombat's Delicacy

Preparation Time: 15 mins　　**Cooking Time:** 20 mins　　**Serves:** 2

STEP 1 To make the sauce; melt butter in the base of a grill dish and add lemon juice, parsley, sweet chilli sauce, tomato sauce and the finely chopped onion and mix through. Add in Worcestershire sauce, thousand island dressing, the lemon and dill sauce, minced garlic, French dressing and white wine.

STEP 2 Place fish fillets into the grill dish basting both sides in the sauce. Cook under a medium to hot grill until the fish is cooked through to the centre.

STEP 3 Add a sprinkle of flaked almonds halfway through cooking.

STEP 4 Serve the fish with fresh, steamed vegetables and garnished with parsley.

HINT Use the deep section of the grill dish, keeping juices around fillets as tightly as possible. (A flat dish that spreads the juices is not desirable.) Use good white wine. Fish should not be allowed to dry out. Make sure wine and sauces are sufficient to almost gel to a light gravy when fish is cooked. Depending on fillet sizes, amounts of sauces required may vary. Trial and error will perfect this. If adventurous, drink rest of bottle of wine while cooking or with the meal.

Ingredients
- 2 fillets of fish
- 2 lemons (zested)
- 1 small onion
- 1 tablespoon Worcestershire sauce
- 2 tablespoons thousand island dressing
- 2 tablespoons lemon and dill sauce
- 2 teaspoons garlic (minced)
- 1 tablespoon French dressing
- 3 tablespoons sweet chilli sauce
- 1 tablespoon tomato sauce
- ½ glass good white wine
- parsley (finely chopped)
- flaked almonds
- butter (enough to lightly cover base of dish when melted)

DESSERT

LEMON TART WITH STRAWBERRY SALSA

★ Dana's Deluge

Preparation Time: 10 mins   **Cooking Time:** 20 mins   Serves: 2

STEP 1 Place the sugar, butter, lemons and eggs in a pan over a low heat.

STEP 2 Whisk all ingredients until mixed through to a custard thickness. Place in fridge to cool.

STEP 3 Finely chop the strawberries and mint and mix together.

STEP 4 Put the cooled lemon curd in the tartlet cases and place the strawberry salsa on top. Serve with ice-cream or fresh whipped cream.

HINT When making the lemon curd; if you want it to set, put a teaspoon of cornflour in before cooking, or put a little gelatine in when you put it in the fridge. Otherwise, put it in the fridge for an hour or more.

Ingredients
- 2 lemons (juiced and zested)
- 115g butter
- 170g caster sugar
- 1 punnet strawberries
- 3 eggs
- 1 bunch mint
- 2 tart cases

96

KEWCO QUEENS

Kewco is a long-standing family business manufacturing and retailing bathroom products. Kewco was established 55 years ago by Keri and Lyndall's dad. We thought it would be a great idea to enter a work team so, along with Sue and Irene who are employed in the business, we set off preparing our plan of attack. It has been so much fun establishing our strategy for the competition and we have had many laughs over a spot of wine whilst concocting our recipe plans.

Dad is now retired from the business, however comes in daily to keep in touch and help out where needed. He is one in a million but, devastatingly, is struggling with both prostrate and bone cancer – it really made his day to come to the *Great Aussie Cook Off* to see his 'Kewco Queens'. Dad has brought us lunch every day since we started working for him 27 years ago now – that's a lot of lunches! All the girls get a treasured kiss from him every morning when he comes into work. Not a lot of bosses can get away with that! That's why we're called the 'Kewco Queens'. He makes us feel like royalty.

We love getting together as a family and given there are 18 grandchildren, one great grandchild and 13 adults – our gatherings are certainly not a small affair. As the years go by we find that our cooking experiences form a major topic of conversation at any family gathering. We are always swapping our recipes and sharing our latest cooking experiences. It really is the great common denominator amongst us all.

Team Members: Sue Haggatt, Lyndall Walter, Keri Bryant, Irene Fochtman.

ENTRÉE

HONEY SOY CHICKEN SKEWERS
SERVED WITH ASIAN SALAD AND COUSCOUS

★ Sue's Skewers

Preparation Time: 20 mins   **Cooking Time:** 15 mins   **Serves:** 2

STEP 1 Marinate chicken thighs in a mixture of honey, soy sauce and mixed herbs. Skewer marinated chicken and cook thoroughly in a frying pan.

STEP 2 Mix together ingredients for the Asian salad in a bowl. Mix sweet chilli sauce, soy sauce, fish sauce and coriander into a dressing and toss through the salad.

STEP 3 Prepare the couscous as per instructions on the packet. Add grated lemon, lightly browned almond flakes, crispy diced bacon rashers, cooked spring onions and diced capsicum.

STEP 4 Just before serving, heat through couscous on low heat and spoon into a cup/ramekin. Fill to the top and turn upside down on plate. Serve immediately with the chicken skewers and Asian salad.

Ingredients
2 chicken thighs
4 tablespoons honey
4 tablespoons soy sauce
2 tablespoon mixed herbs

Asian salad
½ cabbage (finely shredded)
2 cups baby spinach (finely shredded)
1 carrot (grated)
¼ capsicum (finely sliced)
½ cup bean shoots
4 tablespoons sweet chilli sauce
2 tablespoons fish sauce
2 teaspoons coriander

Couscous
½ cup lemon zest
½ cup almond flakes
½ cup diced capsicum
½ cup spring onions
½ cup crispy, diced bacon rashers

MAIN

FLAVOURED KING GEORGE WHITING
WITH GARLIC SAUCE

★ Peninsula Delight

Preparation Time: 30 mins   **Cooking Time:** 20 mins   **Serves:** 2

STEP 1 For the garlic sauce; melt butter in a frying pan and add the cornflour. Stir for approximately 1 minute on medium heat. Add the garlic and garlic salt to taste. Whisk lightly until thickened.

STEP 2 For the side dish; heat a frying pan and add butter and carrots, stirring for 1 minute. Add bok choy and basil, stirring for 1 minute. Heat some oil in a separate frying pan and pan fry potatoes until crisp. Set aside.

STEP 3 Coat fish fillets with lemon pepper and plain flour. Heat oil in shallow frying pan and panfry for 1 minute on each side.

STEP 4 Plate up the fish, garnished with lemon wedges, and place on top of bok choy and carrots with the crisp potatoes scattered across top. Spoon garlic sauce over the fish.

HINT Ensure fish is as fresh as possible – maybe even catch your own!

Ingredients
4 King George whiting fillets
4 tablespoons lemon pepper
plain flour for dusting
oil for shallow frying
lemon wedges

Garlic sauce
2 teaspoons butter
2 teaspoons cornflour
1 cup of milk
crushed garlic & garlic salt to taste

Side Dish
2 boiled potatoes (coarsely diced)
1 small carrot (cut into thin strips)
2 bunches bok choy
½ cup fresh basil
1 teaspoon butter
oil for shallow frying

DESSERT

BERRY PANCAKES
★ Berry Bliss

| **Preparation Time:** 10 mins | **Cooking Time:** 5 mins | **Serves:** 1 |

STEP 1 Sift flour, sugar and bicarbonate soda into bowl, make a well in centre and pour in whisked egg and milk. Combine and blend until smooth.

STEP 2 Preheat frying pan, add butter to heat and spoon out batter making into circles in the frying pan. Wait for bubbles to appear on the batter and then flip over.

STEP 3 Top with pre-frozen/fresh mixed berries, fresh strawberries, dollop of cream, dust with icing sugar and spoon strawberry puree around the edges of the plate.

HINT Typically use ½ cup batter for larger pancakes. This recipe can have many variations for the toppings. Examples: use lemon and sugar; jam and ice-cream.

Ingredients
1 cup self raising flour
1 egg
¼ cup caster sugar
¼ teaspoon bicarbonate soda
¾ cup milk
butter
pre-frozen/fresh mixed berries,
punnet fresh strawberries
cream
icing sugar
strawberry puree to serve

TEAM BINDAAS

The word 'Bindaas' comes from India and in Hindi language it means being carefree, powerful yet easy going, jolly people with a positive attitude. Bindaas also means extra-ordinary people with lots of fun and happiness.

Our team is a group of Bindaas people who are housemates, neighbours and friends. The food we cook comes from different regions however each of us has India as our heritage. We grew up in India where our parents, siblings and relatives still live today. Our ancestors also lived in India and we have heard many amazing and interesting stories from their time.

Whilst each of us lived in India, it was Australia that brought us together. We have all lived here for a number of years and met over a year ago in Brisbane. It is no surprise that our cooking style is highly influenced by traditional Indian cooking – authentic ingredients, methods and tastes. Our inspiration however comes from keeping a balanced state of wellbeing. Our Mothers passed down the fine art and secret tips that make Indian food an awesome dining experience. Secrets like using all your senses during cooking not just taste, the way you can smell whether the food is cooked, or how the colour can determine its cooking time.

Our cooking passions include experimenting with recipes, learning new dishes, inviting friends over, having fun and sharing in the joy of food. Our speciality is authentic Indian, pure vegetarian, gluten-free, highly nutritious and easy to cook. We wish to share love and happiness through our food and with the many friends from all cultures of which we have made here in Australia.

Team Members: Kiran Ramanahalli, Rinkle Shah, Vineeta Lal, Ajit Jain

ENTRÉE

POTATO BHAJIYA AND CHUTNEY

★ Rinkle's hot potato bhaji

Preparation Time: 5 mins   **Cooking Time:** 10 mins   **Serves:** 2

STEP 1 Add the chilli powder, garam masala, turmeric, salt and pepper to the bowl of chick pea flour add the water and mix well to form consistent batter. Set aside for 2 minutes.

STEP 2 Heat a cup of sunflower oil in a large frying pan for 2–3 minutes so it is ready for deep frying. Once the oil is heated turn to medium heat for frying. Dip the circularly cut potato pieces into the batter and place them in the frying pan. Cook for about 30 seconds on each side until they are golden brown. Deep fried bhajiyas are now ready to serve.

STEP 3 To make the chutney mix all the coriander, green chillies, mint leaves, yoghurt, salt and lemon in a blender. The chutney is ready to serve.

STEP 4 Serve the hot golden brown potato bhajiya with chutney, tomato sauce, hot chilli sauce or sweet chilli sauce depending on your tastes and preferences.

HINT Oil should be well heated before placing the potato batter into the frying pan. To test whether the oil is heated well or not, put a pinch of batter in the heating oil. If it comes to the surface, the oil is ready for frying if not leave longer. Vegetable oil can also be used instead of olive oil for this dish.

Ingredients

- 1 cup sunflower oil
- 1 cup chick pea flour
- 1 potato (peeled and sliced into circular thin pieces)
- pinch chilli powder
- pinch garam masala
- pinch turmeric
- salt and pepper to taste
- ¾ cup water

Chutney
- 300g coriander
- 4 green chillies
- 200g mint leaves
- 5 tablespoons spoons plain yoghurt
- salt and lemon to taste

CHHOLE CHAWAL

★ Vineeta and Kiran's combo chhole chawal

Preparation Time: 7 mins **Cooking Time:** 15 mins **Serves:** 2

STEP 1 *Chawal:* Heat ghee in a frying pan, add cumin seeds, bay leaves, cloves and cashews. Sauté on a low temperature for approximately 1 minute till the cashews are golden brown. Add washed basmati rice, water and salt to the frying pan and mix.

STEP 2 Place mixture in a microwave safe bowl and cook in the microwave covered for 12–15 minutes.

STEP 3 *Chhole:* Heat ghee in a wok, add chopped chillies, garlic, ginger and onion. Fry the mix on medium temperature for 2–3 minutes until golden brown. Add tomatoes, turmeric powder, chilli powder, coriander powder, garam masala, dry fenugreek leaves and salt to taste. Sauté until tomatoes are soft and curry is formed. Add 2–5 spoons of water in case the mix sticks to the surface of the wok. Stir while cooking to ensure well blended for a further 2–3 minutes.

STEP 4 Add chick peas and water to the curry and boil for 3 minutes.

STEP 5 Serve hot with Chawal and garnish with freshly chopped coriander.

HINT This dish is a combination of north and south India. Fresh lemon juice can be added in chhole while serving for those who like a little sour taste.

Ingredients

Chawal
1 cup basmati rice
¼ cup ghee
cumin seeds
1 bay leaf
2 cloves
5 cashews (halved)
salt to taste
2 cups water

Chhole
canned chick peas
1 onion (chopped)
1 tomato (chopped)
½ thumb size ginger (chopped)
3 chillies (chopped)
2 garlic cloves (chopped)
1 pinch turmeric powder
½ teaspoon chilli powder
½ teaspoon coriander powder
1 pinch garam masala
dry fenugreek leaves
salt to taste
¼ cup ghee

DESSERT

SHEERA
★ Ajit's Shaahi Sheera

Preparation Time: 2 mins   **Cooking Time:** 7 mins   **Serves:** 2

STEP 1 Heat ghee in frying pan and add semolina. Roast at a low temperature for 3–4 minutes until golden brown. Keep stirring to avoid sticking to the pan base.

STEP 2 Add raw sugar, warm water, cardamom powder and saffron. Mix well and stir for 3–4 minutes.

STEP 3 Serve hot and garnish with almonds.

HINT Soak almonds in warm water from 2 hours or over night to make them soft and easier to chop. Shaahi means Royal. This is the traditional Royal Indian dessert, which is prepared on every auspicious occasion throughout India. This recipe was passed down from our mother as it is prepared by all the families.

Ingredients
½ cup ghee
½ cup raw sugar
½ cup semolina
1 cup warm water
1–2 cardamoms or cardamom powder
3–4 chopped almonds
1 pinch saffron

BELLE ITALIANI FAMILY

Coming from an Italian background has been interesting, but growing up wasn't so easy. My parents made everything from homemade olives, salami, prosciutto, sauce, pasta and pizza. While my friends went to the beach on weekends, my sister, brother and I had to stay home and make tomato sauce. Our picnics weren't like the average Australian's - there was no such thing as a barbeque or take-away in our household! Mum would cook pasta and we would bring that to the picnic and to me that was normal. Learning how to roll out pasta with a one meter stick took a lot of practice. Thank God for technology.

These days some things have changed. I do buy take-away. I don't make my own tomato paste (my parents curse me) but I do make my own bolognese sauce. I don't roll out pasta, but I do use my pasta machine. If you walk into my parents' garage you will still see their salami hanging from the ceiling - 55 years in Australia hasn't changed them! Mum and Dad still go to my auntie's house and bake 20kilos of pizza and bread in the home-made oven to take.

I thank my Mum today for everything. I try and keep up the Italian traditions. My children love Italian food, especially lasagna, cannelloni and our famous Christmas specialty, chocolate ravioli. I am now passing these traditions down to my own children. My daughter Adriana's turning out to be a very good cook and she intends to be a cooking teacher. Hopefully, the traditions will live on.

Team Members:
Lorri Manfredi,
Sandy Iskra,
Adriana Manfredi,
Terrie Manfredi

ENTRÉE

GARLIC PRAWNS
★ Pino's Prawns

Preparation Time: 10 mins　　**Cooking Time:** 20 mins　　**Serves:** 1

STEP 1 In a saucepan, fry the oil and garlic on a low heat.

STEP 2 Add the canned tomatoes and chilli and cook for at least 10 minutes. Add the prawns and cook through.

STEP 3 Add the chopped parsley just before serving (Serve with bread on the side)

HINT When adding the tomatoes to the saucepan, make sure it has cooled down first otherwise it will spit everywhere.

Ingredients
8 green prawns (shelled and deveined)
1 tablespoon garlic paste
2 tablespoons hot chilli paste
1 tablespoon fresh parsley
1 x 400g can peeled tomatoes
3 tablespoons oil

MAIN

GRILLED CHICKEN WITH HERBED BREADCRUMBS

★ Lorri's Chicken

Preparation Time: 10 mins   **Cooking Time:** 20 mins   **Serves:** 1

STEP 1 Salt the chicken.

STEP 2 Put bread crumbs, parsley, pepper and Italian herbs into a bowl. Mix in the oil and vinegar, making sure mixture is moist.

STEP 3 Spread the mixture onto the chicken breast.

STEP 4 Cook the chicken on a grill, on low heat, so it cooks slowly all the way through. The chicken is ready when the bread crumbs are golden in colour.

STEP 5 Serve with fresh salad or steamed vegetables.

HINT Make sure the bread is at least 2–3 days old.

Ingredients
1 chicken breast (skinless)
1 cup fresh bread crumbs (use bread 2–3 days old and crumble with hands)
3 tablespoons oil
1 tablespoon white vinegar
salt
pepper to taste
1 teaspoon mixed Italian herbs
1 teaspoon parsley (chopped)

DESSERT

LA TAZZA DOLCE

★ Adriana's dessert

Preparation Time: 10 mins   **Cooking Time:** 20 mins   **Serves:** 1

STEP 1 Place the chocolate in a double sauce pan. (Water at the bottom and chocolate on the top). Heat the water until the chocolate melts. Take off the heat and stand to cool.

STEP 2 While waiting for the chocolate to cool, blow up the balloon and tie it up.

STEP 3 To make saucer, place melted chocolate onto baking paper, spread it with a spatula just enough so you can shape your saucer.

STEP 4 Just before it sets, use a glass and shape your saucer, press firmly and let it set completely.

STEP 5 Dip your balloon into the melted chocolate (about $1/3$ of the way) let your balloon set onto baking paper.

STEP 6 Shape the handle of the cup with a piping bag onto the baking paper.

STEP 7 When the chocolate has set, release the air from the balloon.

STEP 8 Add a bit of melted chocolate so you can attach the handle and the cup to the saucer.

STEP 9 Fill cup with mousse and decorate with whipped cream and a strawberry.

Ingredients
375g block dark cooking chocolate
1 balloon
1 teaspoon whipped cream
1 cup ready-made chocolate mousse
1 strawberry

HINT When dipping balloon into melted chocolate make sure chocolate has cooled down.

THE SUPER STORMS

Our family history is one of self-sufficiency and adaptations. We love to cook because we are all artists in our own way and creativity comes out in all aspects of our life. Our cooking is inspired by our environment and is both imaginative and practical. Living a very busy life, quick and easy, yet nutritious meals are a necessity.

We like to be adventurous and spontaneous, often producing the same meals with a different twist. We all have different palates so eating in our house is complex but entertaining. Brieanna is a meat eater and savoury child with lactose intolerance, Cheyvonne and Meachelle like vegetarian and seafood orientated food and Shonae prefers sweet, basic foods yet also likes to have a combination of traditional European and Asian dishes. Compromise and variety is mandatory. Our signature dish is French toast, something we all enjoy, and can all make easily!

Our heritage is extremely diverse. Together our ancestry is of European, Polish, Irish, American, the United Kingdom, Australian and Aboriginal descent. Despite all these influences, our palates and a large variety of cookbooks primarily determine our cooking choices. We are developing our own unique heritage and hopefully the girls will continue to influence future generations with a desire to try all types of meals from all nationalities.

Team Members:
Cheyvonne Sauer
Shonae Morrison,
Brieanna Sauer,
Meachelle Morrison,

ENTRÉE

ZESTY VEGETABLE TEMPURA
AND HERBED RICE

★ Hail Storm

Preparation Time: 10 mins **Cooking Time:** 20 mins **Serves:** 4

STEP 1 Place the rice in a microwave bowl with 3 cups of water. Cook covered for 12 minutes and then stand aside to rest.

STEP 2 Blend the flour, 1 cup of water, egg and mixed spice together until smooth.

STEP 3 Add 1 cup of water to a wok or frying pan on high heat and bring to boil. Add the vegetables and blanch for 2–3 minutes until they just start to tenderise. (Can also be done in microwave).

STEP 4 Add 2 cups of oil in deep saucepan on high heat. Test if oil is heated by adding a small amount of batter mix to see if cooks quickly. The batter will form a small solid shape and rise to the top of the oil with bubbles around it when it is ready to use.

STEP 5 Dip vegetables and fruit into batter, coating well then cook in the oil until golden. Remove the fruit and vegetables and allow to drain on wire rack.

STEP 6 Mix the herbs and rice together. Serve the tempura atop a bed of rice. Drizzle prepared Maggi Zesty Sauce over the rice and tempura.

Ingredients

1 cup self raising flour
1 teaspoon mixed spice
1 egg
2 cups oil
1–2 cups fresh fruit and vegetables strawberries, banana, rockmelon, broccoli, cauliflower, carrot strips and baby corn
1 cup balsamati rice
¼ cup finely chopped fresh herbs parsley, mint, and lemongrass
½ cup Maggi Zesty Citrus sauce
4 cups water

HINT Use long tongs and a long drainage sieve to assist in safety control when cooking the fruit and vegetables in the oil.

MAIN

MEAT AND VEGE BOULDERS WITH SALSA

★ Earthquake

Preparation Time: 15 mins **Cooking Time:** 20 mins **Serves:** 4

STEP 1 Mix all boulder ingredients together in a bowl.

STEP 2 Form boulders in microwave egg bowls and cook in the microwave on high for approximately 1–2 minutes until cooked through, time will vary according to microwave. They should appear lightly coloured throughout and fats are separated.

STEP 3 Remove boulders from bowls, use the fats in the bowl to assist in searing them in a frying pan, low grill plate or BBQ. On high heat cook for approximately 1 minute. This is simply to brown them, and remove any extra fats. Set aside in an oven on low heat to keep warm until serving.

STEP 4 Put topping ingredients into frying pan and cook on a high heat for 2 minutes. Set aside.

STEP 5 Mix all salsa ingredients together and cook over medium heat for approximately 3 minutes until well combined.

STEP 6 To serve layer the salsa on the base of the plate, place the boulders on top and then topping over the boulders.

HINT Mince could be of any meat/seafood or vegetarian varieties or tofu.

Ingredients

Boulders
- 250g mince
- ½ cup diced red pepper
- ¼ cup peas
- ½ cup bread crumbs (or 2 slices bread crust grated)
- ½ cup processed bran (optional)
- ¼ cup bean sprouts
- 2 eggs
- ½ cup shredded cheese (own choice)
- ½ cup grated carrot
- 1 teaspoon mild chilli
- 1 tablespoon Italian herbs

Topping
- 2 cups shredded cabbage
- 1 tablespoon garlic granules
- 1 cup water

Salsa
- ½ cup diced tomato
- ¼ cup diced gherkin
- ¼ cup onion
- ½ cup corn relish

DESSERT

MOCHA SUNDAE

★ Volcanic Eruption

Preparation Time: 10–15 mins   **Cooking Time:** nil   **Serves:** 2

STEP 1 Cut pointed end off ice-cream cones and coat with ice magic, allow to set.

STEP 2 Fill cone ends with choice of filling and seal with a marshmallow and more ice magic.

STEP 3 Turn the cone end upside down onto mini wagon wheel biscuit and join with more ice magic and decorate with 100's and 1000's or chocolate flakes.

STEP 4 In a parfait glass, place cone, the ice-cream and cover with 100's and 1000's and marshmallows.

STEP 5 Pour in the coffee essence and milk, top with whipped cream and decorate with more ice magic swirls and chocolate flakes or 100's and 1000's. Serve.

Ingredients
2 chocolate mini wagon wheels
2 ice-cream cones
½ cup ice-cream (flavour of choice)
½ cup milk
½ cup marshmallows (mini)
1 teaspoon chickory coffee essence
1 can whipped cream
ice magic (flavour of choice)
fondant/jelly or favourite sauce filling
100's and 1000's or chocolate flakes
icing sugar for dusting

HINT Make the cones ahead of time in bulk and store in an airtight container in the fridge they are great for school lunch treats (if they last that long!).

COOKING CALVERTS

The Calverts go back a long way, in fact we have ancestral connections to the infamous bushranger, Ned Kelly. Julie's grandfather, George Calvert, was a swagman during the depression. When he married Julie's grandmother, May, they did it tough living in a slab bush hut and making ends meet.

Together they raised two sons and five daughters who in turn gave George and May twenty grandchildren. Julie is the eldest and Lucy is the second youngest of this fifth generation of Calverts and now there are countless great-grandchildren. Grandma Calvert was always the matriarch and today at 95 is still nicknamed the "Courier Mail" for her thorough knowledge of what's going on in the world.

Julie and her cousins have fond childhood memories of Grandma's cooking and baking and her father, aunts and uncles have all carried the family cooking flag on to their own families. From sweet baked treats from her grandmother's day, to the savoury, hearty comfort food of her parent's era, the new generation of Calverts has embraced the eclectic Asian and European influences and added another dimension to our families' traditional recipes.

Also of great culinary inspiration to us all, now and in the past, has been our sensational Queensland climate and proximity to Moreton Bay. We would say every one of the Calverts has at some time lived in the South-Eastern bayside suburbs of Brisbane. You can almost taste the sunshine and salty sea in our food.

Team Members:
Lucy Ohl, Gary Waldon, Julie Calvert, Gerry Calvert

ENTRÉE

SPICY CALAMARI
AND FRESH HERB SALAD

★ Calamari 'Bash'

Preparation Time: 30 mins   **Cooking Time:** 10 mins   **Serves:** 4

STEP 1 Prepare the squid by removing head and tentacles from tube. Cut the tube down one side and then into small pieces of approximately 5cm x 5cm. Remove the gut, beak and eyes from the head. Rinse all pieces and dry with paper towel.

STEP 2 Using a meat mallet, bash the individual pieces until well pulped.

STEP 3 Prepare the herb salad by combining salad and herb leaves and cucumber in a small bowl and toss together. In a clean jar or shaker, add all dressing ingredients and shake vigorously to combine. Set aside until step 6.

STEP 4 Finely dice the capsicum, tomato and shallots. Combine together with the garlic, lemongrass, coriander and chilli in a frying pan with the oil and fry on a medium heat until browned. (You could also use a camp fire or BBQ plate).

STEP 5 Lightly dust all pieces of squid with plain flour and add to the frying pan and continue to cook with the other ingredients on medium heat, turning frequently for a further 5 minutes or until squid has just firmed up. Add the fish sauce and lemon juice to mix 2 minutes before the squid has finished cooking.

STEP 6 Add salad dressing to bowl of salad herbs and toss. Pile mounds of herb salad onto each plate and top with the spicy squid mix. Serve with lemon wedges on the side.

Ingredients
800g small squid, cuttle fish or baby octopus
1 small red capsicum
1 small tomato
6 shallots
2 tablespoons vegetable oil for frying
1 dessertspoon fish sauce
2 teaspoons crushed garlic
1–2 teaspoons lemongrass
1–2 teaspoons coriander (chopped)
1 teaspoon chilli
½ cup plain flour
½ lemon (juiced)

Herb salad ingredients
2 large handfuls mixed salad leaves
½ cup coriander leaves
½ cup mint leaves
1 small cucumber (peeled and shaved into strips with vegetable peeler. Discard seeds and pulp)

Dressing Ingredients
2 tablespoons lime juice
2 tablespoons peanut oil
2 tablespoons light soy sauce
¼ teaspoon sesame oil
1 teaspoon chilli
1 teaspoon ginger

HINT Ensure the squid pieces are bashed to an almost unrecognisable pulp. Beware, any on lookers could get splattered!

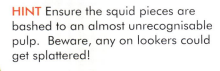

MAIN

OYSTER PIES

★ Gerry's 'Spare' Oyster Pies

| Preparation Time: 20 mins | Cooking Time: 30 mins | Serves: 4 |

STEP 1 Place the butter, cheddar cheese, pepper, garlic and fish sauce in medium saucepan and cook over medium heat until golden in colour. (Don't worry if it sticks to the pan, as it will dissolve when the milk is added.

STEP 2 Add the plain flour and cook without stirring for 1 minute before mixing into a gooey mess.

STEP 3 Add the cream cheese, milk, water from the oysters and lemongrass to create cheese rue sauce. Turn the heat to low and using a potato masher, scrape the cheese off the bottom of the saucepan and continue to mash and scrape until the mixture returns to thickened rue. This will not happen until the sauce nears boiling point again.

STEP 4 Remove from heat and refrigerate until cold. See hints.

STEP 5 Line 4 large muffin tins with puff pastry. It is easier to cut pastry strips to line around the side of the muffin tin and then a circle for the bottom and a larger circle of pastry for the pie lid after filling.

STEP 6 Drain and add oysters to the cold rue, stir gently and spoon into pie cases, each pie needs 2 or 3 oysters or if it is easier the oysters may be added directly to the pie on top of the sauce rather than first mixing them into the rue.

STEP 7 Cover the pie cases with the larger circle of pastry and pinch the edges with your fingers to seal in the filling. Lay a few small left over pastry scraps decoratively across the top of each pie

STEP 8 Cook in a hot oven (220°C) for 15 –20 minutes. Serve the pies with a fresh green salad on the side.

Ingredients
1 jar of 10–12 fresh oysters in sea water
2 sheets puff pastry
50g cream cheese
20g mature cheddar cheese
1 cup milk
½ of oyster water from the jar
1 tablespoon butter
1 heaped tablespoon plain flour
1 teaspoon garlic
1 teaspoon lemongrass
2 teaspoons fish sauce
cracked black pepper

HINT It is preferable that the oysters not be too cooked in the pie, so first refrigerate the cheese rue sauce to cold before adding the oysters and assembling the pies. Using a cold rue will also prevent the pie contents from overflowing whilst in the oven.

DESSERT

BANANA SPRING ROLLS
WITH PALM SUGAR CARAMEL

★ Julie's Gone Bananas

Preparation Time: 10 mins **Cooking Time:** 20 mins **Serves:** 4

STEP 1 In a small non-stick saucepan, add butter, palm sugar and pouring cream. Gently bring to the boil while stirring and cook until slightly thickened. Remove from the heat and set caramel aside to cool slightly.

STEP 2 Cut each banana in half and wrap in pastry like a parcel, each half in it's own sheet of pastry. Combine salsa ingredients and set aside

STEP 3 Heat the oil in a frying pan to a heat where the spring rolls can turn golden brown slowly. (See hint below). Shallow fry each of the banana rolls in batches, turning on all sides until golden. Remove and place on paper towel to absorb the excess oil.

STEP 4 Cut each banana spring roll in half diagonally and drizzle the caramel over the top and dust with icing sugar. Serve with a dollop of cream, scoop of ice cream and strawberry salsa on the side.

HINT To test the temperature of the oil fry a small piece of leftover pastry. It should sizzle but not brown too quickly.

Ingredients

4 ripe cavendish bananas
8 sheets ready-made spring roll pastry
40g butter
300g dark palm sugar (or brown sugar)
¾ cup pouring cream
1 tablespoon icing sugar
vegetable oil (fill the frying pan to 1cm in depth)
double cream and vanilla ice-cream to serve

Strawberry and mint salsa
1 punnet ripe strawberries (hulled and finely chopped)
10 fresh mint leaves (finely chopped)

THE CAMPBELL COOKING CREW

With a surname like Campbell our family background has to hail from Scotland. My grandfather immigrated to Australia after being a pilot in the RAF. After settling in Warwick he and his wife moved to Brisbane about the time that I was born. My wife's grandparents ironically were also from Warwick. My wife and I met through Scouting and my first Cub Leader is now my Father-in-law.

My father decided to open a restaurant with my uncle in the early 1970's. It was called *The Fiveways* located south of the city of Brisbane. It is here where I first remember the hustle and bustle of a kitchen and the goings on of a busy restaurant. They moved to another venture in the 1980's with the *Clansmen Restaurant* at Annerley where I worked as a dishwasher and barman. After helping in the cold larder section a few times I really loved to watch food being created.

Food was always part of our lives as we sampled other establishments fare at least once a week. I prefer the family style of cooking at home as it brings everyone together and dining out these days is quite expensive. The meal I remember most is Dad's bacon and tomato on toast for Sunday night dinner after a busy weekend at the restaurant. Sadly my father passed away suddenly in 2002, but I still like to recreate that meal.

When I was a teenager my Mother wouldn't allow me to enter the kitchen, so I try to involve my own six children in the processes and teaching them what I have learned. I enjoy cooking for my wife and our children at night when I come home. It relaxes me and I can forget about the grind at work and create something from nothing.

Team Members:
Emily, Matthew,
Amy, Holly

ENTRÉE

PUMPKIN AND SWEET POTATO SOUP
IN BREAD ROLL WITH CORIANDER SOUR CREAM AND CAMEMBERT DIPPERS

★ Golden Silk and cheese fingers

Preparation Time: 5 mins   **Cooking Time:** 15 mins   **Serves:** 2

STEP 1 To steam the vegetables add pumpkin and sweet potato to a steamer, use the chicken stock for steaming liquid, add garlic to the stock and then steam for 12 minutes.

STEP 2 When the vegetables are cooked through, place in a blender with half of the used hot stock and the vegemite. Puree till smooth. In a separate bowl, mix sour cream and coriander.

STEP 3 Cut the camembert into strips and breadcrumb both sides. In a nonstick frying pan (add oil if not non stick) fry the cheese until golden on both sides.

STEP 4 Remove the top off the bread rolls and hollow out the middle. Pour soup into hollow of the bread roll and top with sour cream and coriander. Serve with Camembert dippers.

HINT Place bread roll under grill after hollowing out, so the bottom does not go soggy.

Ingredients
2 cups raw butternut pumpkin (chopped in small cubes)
1 cup raw sweet potato (chopped in small cubes)
1 teaspoon minced garlic
400ml chicken stock
½ teaspoon vegemite
2 crusty bread rolls hollowed out with top off
200ml sour cream
1 teaspoon fresh coriander (chopped)
1 small round camembert cheese (cut into strips)
breadcrumbs

MAIN

SALMON FILLET
WRAPPED IN ROSEMARY AND GARLIC INFUSED PROSCIUTTO SERVED WITH BLANCHED GREEN BEANS AND TWICE COOKED BABY POTATOES

★ Winter Fish Dish

Preparation Time: 10 mins   **Cooking Time:** 25 mins   **Serves:** 2

STEP 1 Boil the potatoes in salted water. Remove when tender and drain well.

STEP 2 Mix rosemary and garlic together in cup and brush on both sides of the prosciutto. Wrap the prosciutto around the middle of the salmon fillet. Fry on one side on a medium heat for 3 minutes or until golden. When cooked half way through, cover with foil and place in moderate oven for 8 minutes.

STEP 3 Place potatoes in a frying pan with olive oil and cook until golden brown.

STEP 4 Blanch beans in hot water or steam for 2 minutes and serve immediately with salmon and potatoes.

Ingredients
2 salmon fillets (boned with skin on or off)
2 slices prosciutto
1 tablespoon spoon rosemary
1 tablespoon minced garlic
6 baby potatoes
1 handful of green beans topped and tailed

HINT Add salt to potatoes before baking Serve with Mahito Mum's favourite drink.

DESSERT

FRUIT KEBAB TOTEM
WITH GINGER AND HONEY YOGHURT

★ Yum Yum Sticks

Preparation Time: 10 mins **Cooking Time:** 10 mins **Serves:** 2

STEP 1 Add juice of 1 lime to chopped banana.

STEP 2 Place one of each fruit piece on kebab stick. Mix the yoghurt, honey and ginger together in a small bowl.

STEP 3 Use a wedge of lime to create centre point for totem and place a strawberry on top. Place small bowl of dipping yoghurt under the Totem.

HINT The lime stops the banana from going brown as well as tasting good.

Ingredients
1 punnet fresh strawberries
1 banana chopped into 2cm chunks
1 mandarin portioned in pieces
1 kiwi fruit peeled and quartered
1 cup pineapple chopped into bite sized chunks
1 lime juiced
1 lime cut into wedges
250ml plain Greek yoghurt
2 tablespoons honey
1 teaspoon ginger

GROOVY GRANDMAS

Bryony Preece lives in beautiful Nelson Bay with her children living two hours away in Sydney. When Bryony's husband, Colin, died two and a half years ago, long-term friends Vicki and Carol, and her other groovy girlfriends became her local "family".

Most of Bryony's friends where already grandmothers, so when her daughter Vanessa announced she was pregnant it strengthened their bond and was the catalyst for the website, "Groovy Grandmas". That was how we all met.

A year later Groovy Grandmas had so many fabulous stories from around Australia that we decided to self-publish an annual calendar and put ourselves on the front cover. That's how we became The Groovy Grandma Cover Girls.

The four of us are very different: different personalities, shapes, sizes and lifestyles, but all are of the same heritage. We are all Aussie baby boomers - born in the 1950's and growing up in Australia in the 1960s and 1970s. We are the surfie chicks, the hippie chicks, the super mums of the seventies and now, thanks to our children, the groovy grandmas of the 21st century.

We love cooking because we all love eating and sharing time together. We get a kick out of seeing our blended recipe versions and inventions enjoyed by our families and loved ones. Together we create a cooking style which is "Retro with a twist" and extremely groovy.

Team Members: Carol Clima, Beth Parkinson, Bryony Preece, Vicki Ashford.

ENTRÉE

SALSA OYSTERS WITH CUCUMBER SANDWICHES

★ Twisted Oysters Groovy Grandma Style

Preparation Time: 10 mins   **Cooking Time:** nil   **Serves:** 1

STEP 1 Arrange oysters in half shells on a serving plate.

STEP 2 Combine salsa ingredients in a mixing bowl. Mix then spoon evenly onto each of the oysters.

STEP 3 Prepare the cucumber sandwiches by placing the thin slices of cucumber on the buttered bread. Remove the crusts and cut into equal serves.

STEP 4 Place the sandwiches on the plate with the oysters and garnish with the fresh chilli and lime wedges.

HINT Port Stephens has some of the best oyster farming in New South Wales.

Ingredients

6 fresh rock oysters in the shell (preferably Port Stephens) per serve

Salsa

1 small tomato (chopped)
2 tablespoons red capsicum (chopped)
1 spring onion (chopped)
½ teaspoon each garlic, coriander and chilli pastes
lime juice
salt and pepper to taste
fresh chilli and lime wedges to serve

Sandwiches

1 small lebanese cucumber (thinly sliced)
2 slices wholemeal bread (buttered)

MAIN

ALMOND AND PARMESAN CRUSTED CHICKEN KIEV
WITH MASHED POTATO AND SPRING VEGETABLES

★ Groovy Chicken Kiev with a Nutty Twist

Preparation Time: 10 mins   **Cooking Time:** 15 mins   **Serves:** 1

STEP 1 In a small bowl mix together the butter with the garlic paste. Make a small, deep cut in the side of the chicken breast with a sharp knife to form a small pocket. Fill this pocket with half the butter and garlic mixture. Close and seal the opening with a toothpick.

STEP 2 Place the crumb crust ingredients on a shallow dish and toss to mix, seasoning to taste. Mix the egg and milk and lightly beat. Take the prepared chicken breast, dust with the flour and dip in the egg and milk mix then into crumb crust mixture coating the chicken well.

STEP 3 Boil the potatoes. Place the vine-ripened tomatoes on a sheet of baking paper on a baking tray and drizzle with basil paste and a little olive oil. Bake tomatoes in oven on medium 10 minutes.

STEP 4 Heat the oil and remaining garlic butter in a non-stick frying pan on medium heat until the butter is foaming. Cook the chicken over a medium heat turning often to cook evenly on all sides and prevent burning.

STEP 5 Mash the potatoes with extra butter and milk and season to taste.

STEP 6 Serve the chicken with the mashed potatoes, vine-ripened roast tomatoes and steamed asparagus.

HINT The almond parmesan and parsley crust is a delicious alternative to the usual breadcrumbs.

Ingredients
1 small skinless chicken breast
½ cup plain flour
1 egg lightly beaten
1 tablespoon milk
1 tablespoon cooking oil
2 tablespoons butter
1 teaspoon garlic paste
1 teaspoon basil paste
1 medium potato (peeled and diced)
extra milk and butter
½ bunch asparagus spears
6 vine ripened cherry tomatoes
Crumb Crust
½ cup blanched almonds (finely chopped)
½ cup grated parmesan cheese
1 tablespoon chopped parsley

DESSERT

RHUBARB AND APPLE CRUMBLE

★ Carol's Twisted Apple and Rhubarb Crumble

Preparation Time: 5 mins **Cooking Time:** 18 mins **Serves:** 1

STEP 1 Combine apple, orange juice, rhubarb, brown sugar and cinnamon in a microwave safe mixing bowl. Cover with cling wrap and microwave on high for approximately 2–3 minutes until apple and rhubarb are tender.

STEP 2 While the apple is cooking, make the crumble topping. Combine rolled oats, coconut, flour, brown sugar and cinnamon in a bowl. Use finger tips to rub the butter evenly into other combined crumble ingredients.

STEP 3 Remove the cling wrap from the apple and rhubarb mixture and transfer to a ramekin or other small, oven-safe dish.

STEP 4 Top with the crumble mix. Place in oven on medium to hot for 15 minutes until nicely golden. Serve with a dollop of cream and the extra orange zest.

HINT Cooking the apples in the microwave rather than stewing the fruit on the stovetop cuts out a lot of time.

Ingredients
1 granny smith apple (peeled and diced)
½ navel orange juiced
1 stick of rhubarb (chopped in 2 cm lengths)
2 teaspoons brown sugar
¼ teaspoon cinnamon

Crumble topping
3 teaspoons butter
1 tablespoon flour
1 tablespoon rolled oats
1 tablespoon coconut
1 teaspoon orange zest
2 teaspoons brown sugar
fresh cream and extra orange zest to serve.

EADES FAMILY

Our combination of English, Croatian and Australian parents together with our Indian, Pakistan, Irish and Sri Lankan friends have exposed us to a wide range of the world's most exciting flavours, spices and tastes.

As a family we love to cook new, exciting dishes with lots of flavour. We are inspired by the challenge of trying something new. A lot of our cooking originates from the Adriatic town of Makarska in Croatia where Maria's father is from. Family favourites include Nik's own macaroni, fish cooked on the gradela and bread and chicken slowly cooked under the sripnja.

Tim and Sarah-Jane both love the experience of cooking, from preparation to creation to the taste sensation. I think our family loves cooking together because it's a great way for us to share the experience, have some fun and imagine that we are sitting, soaking up the sun in the Adriatic Riviera as we enjoy a traditional meal from the region.

Tony and Maria's mothers have also given us an appreciation of fresh, farmhouse cooking using herbs and ingredients grown from our garden. If it's not fresh forget it! If it's a boring packet mix throw it out! If it's bland and void of real flavour – start again! Herbs, fresh ingredients and a little spice is really where it is all at, especially when it comes to our family kitchen.

Team Members:
Tim, Maria, Tony, Sarah-Jane (front)

ENTRÉE

THAI STYLE SQUID SALAD
★ Tim's Salad with Squid

Preparation Time: 20 mins　　**Cooking Time:** 10 mins　　**Serves:** 2

STEP 1 In a mixing bowl mix together the lime juice, garlic and chilli to create a marinade.

STEP 2 Cut the squid into 5cm pieces and mix into the marinade.

STEP 3 Cut the cucumber down the middle and using a teaspoon, take out the middle seeds. Slice the cucumber diagonally.

STEP 4 Combine the dressing ingredients in a small bowl and set aside.

STEP 5 Heat the olive oil in a frying pan and cook the squid for two minutes on high heat or until soft.

STEP 6 Mix the squid with the dressing, then add the coriander, mint, shallot and sesame seeds and serve.

HINT Allow the squid to sit in the marinade for an hour if possible to create a fuller flavour.

Ingredients
- 300g squid
- 1 small Lebanese cucumber
- ½ lime (juiced)
- 1 shallot (sliced)
- 1 clove garlic (crushed)
- ½ red and ½ green chilli (sliced diagonally)
- 2 tablespoons coriander (chopped)
- 3 tablespoons mint (chopped)
- 1 teaspoon sesame seeds
- olive oil

Dressing
- 1 tablespoon lime juice
- ½ tablespoon sweet chilli sauce
- 1 teaspoon fish sauce
- ½ teaspoon brown sugar
- ½ teaspoon sesame oil

MAIN

PRAWNS IN COCONUT MILK

★ Dad's Prawn Moily

Preparation Time: 15 mins **Cooking Time:** 15 mins **Serves:** 2

STEP 1 Heat the oil on high in a frying pan and fry off mustard seeds with curry leaves for about 10 seconds.

STEP 2 Reduce heat and add the ginger, chilli and onion and cook until the onion is brown and soft. Add the tumeric and cubed potato.

STEP 3 Add salt to taste and coconut milk. Simmer for 10 to 15 minutes. Add the basmati rice to a saucepan of boiling water and boil for approx 5 minutes or until cooked.

STEP 4 When the potato is soft add the prawns, cook for 5 minutes and add a squeeze of lemon juice before serving with rice and fresh coriander.

Ingredients

10 to 12 green prawns
1 x 375g tin coconut milk
1 potato (cubed)
½ red chilli (sliced)
½ green chilli (sliced)
½ onion chopped
½ teaspoon black mustard seeds
½ teaspoon yellow mustard seeds
1 stalk curry leaves
2 cloves garlic (crushed)
3cm piece fresh ginger (juilened)
½ teaspoon tumeric
1 teaspoon peanut oil
1 teaspoon lemon juice
1 cup basmati rice
coriander leaves
salt to taste

DESSERT

BANANA SPLIT
WITH CHOCOLATE AND CARAMEL SYRUP

★ Sarah-Jane's Sensational Banana Split

Preparation Time: 10 mins   **Cooking Time:** 5 mins   **Serves:** 1

STEP 1 Melt chocolate in a bowl over a saucepan of boiling water.

STEP 2 Cut the bananas in half and place in a bowl. Add your favourite ice-cream. Top with cream.

STEP 3 Cut the marshmallows into small pieces and sprinkle over the cream.

STEP 4 Drizzle with caramel syrup and sprinkle with nuts and crushed biscuits.

STEP 5 Pour over melted chocolate and top with strawberries.

HINT This is also delicious if topped with seasonal fresh fruits.

Ingredients
50g cooking chocolate
2 bananas
3 marshmallows
2 scoops ice-cream
2 amaretto biscuits (crushed)
2 strawberries
mixed crushed nuts
cream
caramel syrup topping

MACOLINO FAMILY

Gathered around the table you never grow old! This is a strong feeling our family grew up with. Originating from Italy: Veneto on Laura's family side, and Tuscany (with a strong Neapolitan hearth) from Gian Paolo's family side. The flavours from these three Italian regions blend together exquisitely to create a personal touch to all our dishes.

When we moved to Australia two years ago, we discovered that this country had wonderful ingredients we could adapt beautifully to our traditional dishes. We quickly made new friends who love to sit around our dinner table enjoying, tasting and experiencing the new and exciting flavours of our simple and easy cuisine.

Making our own bread, pasta and gnocchi every day is a pleasure we love to share. Friends often come and help cook, ending in hours of fun, chatting and a delicious meal shared together.

When we were little we used to help mum, grandma and all the aunties making lasagne, tagliatelle or ravioli on Sunday mornings. We learnt to cook and started creating our own dishes and this tradition continues in our family with our children.

Grandma Rita, a wonderfully practical country lady from Veneto, used to say: "Bon con bon fa bon," meaning, "Whenever a good ingredient is combined with another good ingredient, the result will be good." We learnt from that!

We remember folding hundreds of tortellini while chatting about relatives and hopes and dreams. Time flew and at the end of the day we all sat around the table happy and exhausted. Being together was priceless!

Team Members:
Gian Paolo,
Laura Corà,
Gaia (front left),
Enrico (front right)

ENTRÉE

TUSCAN SAUSAGE CROSTINI

★ Eat and Go!

Preparation Time: 2 mins   **Cooking Time:** 5 mins   **Serves:** 4

STEP 1 Cut the bread into four slices, 1.5cm thick. Spread a thin layer of garlic on the bread.

STEP 2 Peel the sausages and divide each one into two pieces. Place the sausage on the slices of bread to make a crostino. Place a slice of cheese on top of each crostino.

STEP 3 Put in the oven at 150°C for 5 minutes (or until cheese melts and grills nicely).

HINT You can grill the bread beforehand, for a crunchier taste. Be ready to eat them right away otherwise they'll disappear under your eyes they are delicious. That's why they're called…Eat and Go!

Ingredients

4 slices of Italian style durum wheat bread

2 fresh pork sausages (coarse)

4 slices pecorino cheese (mozzarella can be used instead, or vintage cheddar cheese)

½ teaspoon garlic (crushed)

MAIN

SPRING PASTA WITH INVOLTINI

★ Pasta Mille Colori (Thousand Colours Pasta)

Preparation Time: 10 mins   **Cooking Time:** 15 mins   **Serves:** 4

STEP 1 Boil pasta in 3 litres of water. When water starts to boil add a handful of rocksalt then the pasta immediately. Cook on high heat for 10–12 minutes, adjusting heat so as not to boil over.

STEP 2 Dice vegetables into small pieces. Place them in a pan with the olive oil and Italian herbs and cook them for 10 minutes.

STEP 3 While the vegetables are cooking start preparing the meat involtini. Lay the thin slices of beef on your chopping board. Place on the beef a slice of mortadella and a good pinch of parmesan cheese. Roll them and secure them with a toothpick. Heat a pan and melt the butter with the herbs and rosemary. Place the involtini in the pan and cook for 4 minutes, turning them a few times and adding the wine after the first two minutes.

STEP 4 Drain your pasta, add the vegetables and some more parmesan cheese to taste.

STEP 5 Serve the pasta and involtini together on a plate and garnish the pasta with fresh basil leaves.

HINT Make sure you cook your pasta in enough water, a simple rule is 1 litre of water per 100g pasta, and salt the water.

Ingredients
- 300g pasta shells or fusilli
- 1 tomato, 1 carrot, 1 onion, 1 small capsicum, 1 zucchini, 1 small potato, 150g green beans, ½ an eggplant, 2 cloves garlic
- 60g freshly grated parmesan cheese
- 40g extra virgin olive oil
- 1 teaspoon Italian herbs
- 1 teaspoon mild chilli
- fresh basil leaves to garnish
- handful rocksalt
- pinch salt

Involtini
- 8 slices beef (very finely sliced)
- 8 toothpicks
- 3 slices mortadella (finely sliced)
- 60g freshly grated parmesan cheese
- 40g butter
- 40ml white wine (optional)
- salt and pepper to taste
- 1 teaspoon Italian herbs
- 1 teaspoon rosemary

DESSERT

STRAWBERRY FETTUCCINE

★ Gaia's favourite

Preparation Time: 5 mins   **Cooking Time:** 10 mins   **Serves:** 4

STEP 1 Crush almonds and pistachios separately and set aside.

STEP 2 To prepare crepes, in a blender place eggs, 5g sugar, flour, milk, salt and butter, mix well and set aside for 10 minutes.

STEP 3 Place half the strawberries in a non stick pan with 10g sugar. Cook on low heat for 10 minutes stirring occasionally.

STEP 4 Preheat frying pan and melt butter. Prepare crepes by placing about ¼ of a cup of crepes mixture into the pan. When small bubbles appear on the surface the crepe is ready to be turned. Turn and cook for a further 10 seconds and set aside to cool. Repeat until mixture is finished.

STEP 5 Place cooked strawberries in a mixer and puree. Add pistachio nuts and the rest of the strawberries, finely chopped.

STEP 6 Slice crepes into strips to look like fettuccine. Place them on a serving dish and top with strawberry syrup, strawberries and pistachios. Garnish with finely crushed almonds.

Ingredients

600g strawberries
2 eggs
100g plain flour
250g milk
30g soft butter
15g sugar
50g pistachio nuts
75g almonds (peeled)
pinch salt

HINT Pistachios and almonds can be substituted with other nuts.

MATINAC FAMILY

My cooking style comes from my Croatian, European and Mediterranean background. I was born and raised in Australia. My parents and grandparents are from Bosnia and Croatia. My parents migrated to Australia between the 1960's and 1970's, and both my grandmothers lived in Australia for 12 years. I grew up watching them cook beautiful feasts and learnt from them.

I moved to Croatia when I was 18 years of age which is where I learnt to cook. I loved watching the women cook with fresh meats and vegetables from their own orchards and gardens. It amazed me, and influenced me to cook with fresh ingredients. I had my own chooks, garden, orchard and pigs. Most of my generation will never experience that. I enjoyed every single experience and realised the difference it makes to your cooking.

My inspiration for cooking is seeing everybody enjoy eating my food and being happy and satisfied afterwards. It makes me feel awesome! My family loves cooking simply because we love our food. After a long days work we look forward to having a home cooked meal at the dinner table where we can just talk and relax. There is always plenty of food for everyone to enjoy at my home!

I have travelled with my family to and from Croatia a lot but have finally settled here in Australia. I especially love mixing European and Aussie dishes. There is nothing better than an Aussie BBQ and drinks with Croatian salads and cakes!

Team Members: Klaudia, Ebony, Michelle, Marcia

ENTRÉE

TRADITIONAL CROATIAN SEMOLINA DUMPLING SOUP

★ Svatovska Juha (Wedding Soup)

Preparation Time: 5 mins **Cooking Time:** 10 mins **Serves:** 10

STEP 1 Place the water, salt, pepper, oil, vegetable spice and parsley together in a saucepan and bring to boil.

STEP 2 Lightly beat the egg and add enough semolina to make a thick paste.

STEP 3 As soon as the water mixture begins to boil, using a teaspoon, start scooping small teaspoon size balls of the semolina mixture. Add the balls one by one to the boiling water mixture. Boil for 5 minutes and then turn off the heat. Place a lid on the saucepan and let stand for 5 minutes.

STEP 4 Serve with a dollop of sour cream.

HINT The dumplings will soften and expand when you let the soup stand for 5 minutes with the lid on. You can also add grated carrot and diced potato to this soup, or create a tomato version by adding 3–4 tablespoons of tomato paste.

Ingredients

1 cup semolina flour (enough to make a thick paste)
1 egg
1 teaspoon salt
pinch pepper
1 tablespoon parsley
vegetable spice to taste (VEGETA seasoning stock)
1 litre water
1 tablespoon oil (any)
dollop of sour cream

MAIN

CHICKEN SNITZELS
WITH MASH AND MIXED SALAD

★ Mum's Snitzels

Preparation Time: 10 mins   **Cooking Time:** 10 mins   **Serves:** 8–10

STEP 1 Season the slices of chicken breast with salt, pepper and Vegeta. Place the flour and bread crumbs into separate bowls. Beat the eggs and milk together in another bowl. Crumb the chicken pieces by dipping each piece in the flour, then the milk mixture and finally the bread crumbs. Ensure the chicken is well crumbed. Cover and set aside.

STEP 2 Peel the potatoes and cut into pieces. Boil the potatoes in salted water until soft.

STEP 3 Prepare the salad by placing the sliced onion, cucumber, tomatoes and capsicum into a bowl. Coat with a little oil and add salt and vinegar to taste. Toss the salad gently. Cover and refrigerate.

STEP 4 In a frying pan add oil and heat. Cook the chicken snitzels on a high heat until lightly golden. Drain potatoes and add milk, butter and thickened cream. Mash by hand and then whip the potato mixture with an electric mixer. Season with salt.

STEP 5 Serve the snitzels with the potato mash and mixed salad.

Ingredients
5–6 sliced chicken breasts
1 ½ cups flour
1 ½ cups milk
3 cups breadcrumbs
2 eggs
6 potatoes
¼ cup thickened cream
¼ cup milk
2 tablespoons butter or margarine
1 cucumber (sliced)
2 tomatoes (sliced)
1 yellow, green or red capsicum (sliced)
1 onion (sliced)
oil for frying
vinegar
salt and pepper to taste
vegeta for seasoning (vegetable spice)

HINT Do not cook the snitzels in warm oil otherwise they will go soggy.

DESSERT

CHERRY SLICE CAKE
★ Nana's 'Out on the Ranch' Cherry Slice Cake

Preparation Time: 5 mins **Cooking Time:** 5–10 mins **Serves:** 6–8

STEP 1 Pre-heat the oven to 220°C (fan forced 200°C).

STEP 2 Spray a 23cm x 35cm tin lightly with the oil spray and dust lightly with flour; making sure all of the tin is covered.

STEP 3 Separate the egg whites and egg yolks. In a mixing bowl, use an electric beater to beat the egg whites until very stiff. Mix in the sugar, one tablespoon at a time. Add the egg yolks, one at a time, until just combined. (Do not overmix). Reduce the mixer speed to low and add the flour, 1 tablespoon at a time, and mix until combined.

STEP 4 Place the cake mixture into the cake tin. Scatter the mixture with the cherries. Bake in the oven for 10 minutes, or until the cake is golden brown.

STEP 5 When cooked, remove the cake from the oven and allow to stand for 1 minute before cutting, dusting with icing sugar and serving with fresh cream.

Ingredients
- 5 eggs
- 20 fresh cherries (500g canned or bottled cherries)
- 5 tablespoons plain flour
- 5 tablespoons sugar
- oil spray for lining tin
- extra flour for lining tin
- icing sugar for dusting
- dollop cream or whipped cream

HINT The secret to the cake rising is for the egg whites to be stiff. If you bake this cake in a very hot oven it will only take 10 minutes to cook!

PAKWAAN GROUP

Tathagata Dutta comes from Berhampore (West Bengal), India and is currently working as a Post Doctoral Research Fellow. Lokesh Kaushik comes from a traditional middle class family in a small town of Haryana in India. He is studying Masters of Engineering (software). Ahmed Mehdi comes from the city of mangoes, Multan Pakistan and is currently enrolled in a PhD in Bioinformatics. Malik Adil Nawaz comes from a small town Attock, which is famous for peanuts production near Islamabad, Pakistan. He is currently a student enrolled in Food studies.

With such diverse backgrounds, it is food that brings us together as one. We each share a common passion for cooking. We have been flatmates for almost a year and each enjoy innovation and creativity in the kitchen, constantly developing newer recipes to satisfy our taste buds. We invite our friends over and encourage constructive criticism for each of our creations as this leads to improvements and greater tasting dishes.

Team Members: Malik Adil Nawaz, Tathagata Dutta, Lokesh Kaushik, Ahmed Mehdi

ENTRÉE

TOMATOES' POTTAGE
★ Khati Meethi Tamator Chatni

Preparation Time: 5 mins   **Cooking Time:** 10 mins   **Serves:** 4

STEP 1 Dice tomatoes and finely chop dates and ginger separately.

STEP 2 Pour about ½ cup vegetable oil in a frying pan and heat on medium. Sprinkle finely chopped ginger in the hot oil and fry for 2 minutes.

STEP 4 Add the tomatoes, dates and grapes to the frying pan and fry well (to get homogeneous consistency).

STEP 5 Sprinkle (half teapoon) of salt to the above and add ½ cup of water (to make a thick paste).

STEP 6 Add sugar and mix thoroughly till it becomes viscous (3–5 minutes).

STEP 7 Place on plate, garnish with grapes and serve.

Ingredients
4 fresh tomatoes
25g ginger (finely chopped)
1 cup sugar
¼ cup kishmish (dried grapes)
¼ cup chuharay (dried dates)
½ cup vegetable oil
½ cup water
salt to taste

MAIN

SPICY CHICKPEA WITH PURI

★ Cholay Kararay Aur Puri

Preparation Time: 15 mins **Cooking Time:** 15 mins **Serves:** 4

STEP 1 Pour vegetable oil in a frying pan and heat. Add chopped taka tak (white onions cut in small chunks) and fry till light brown (4–5 minutes).

STEP 2 Add chopped tomatoes and sliced green chilies and cook on medium heat (2–3 minutes).

STEP 3 Add ginger garlic paste and all the spices to the mixture and fry well on medium heat (1–2 minutes).

STEP 4 Add canned chickpeas and fry for another 3 minutes.

STEP 5 Prepare the Puri by adding water slowly to the wheat flour and mixing until it becomes homogeneous.

STEP 5 To prepare the Puri, cover bottom of a frying pan with vegetable oil and heat. Break off a small piece of wheat flour, approximately 50g, using a rolling pin flatten the dough until thin (approximately ½ centimeter thick). Place gently into the hot vegetable oil and deep fry it until it turns light brown (approximately 1 minute). Place on the serving plate (side plate).

STEP 6 Pour chickpea mixture on to a serving plate. Garnish with sliced green chillies, ginger and tomatoes and serve.

Ingredients
400g canned chickpeas
1 fresh tomato (small chunks)
1 large onion (small chunks)
2 fresh green chillies (finely chopped)
1 teaspoon ginger garlic paste
3–4 teaspoons channa massala (spices)
½ teaspoon salt
1 teaspoon red chilli powder
I teaspoon coriander powder
½ teaspoon cumin powder
½ cup vegetable oil

Puri Ingredients
200g wheat flour dough
water
vegetable oil

DESSERT

HALWA

★ Halwa

Preparation Time: 2 mins **Cooking Time:** 7 mins **Serves:** 2

STEP 1 Turn heat to low and add desi ghee in frying pan and heat on high until melted.

STEP 2 Add the semolina and fry until it turns light brown (4–5 minutes).

STEP 3 Add the cashews, almonds and dried grapes (all chopped) to the fried semolina and mix thoroughly (1–2 minutes).

STEP 4 Add 2 cups of water and the sugar to the frying pan and mix over a low heat until the mix becomes semi solid (3–4 minutes).

STEP 5 Place in a bowl and garnish with dry fruits to serve.

Ingredients
100g semolina
½ cup desi (pure) ghee
¼ cup cashews
¼ cup almonds
¼ cup dried grapes
1½ cups sugar
dried fruit mix to garnish

RESOURCE SECTION

CONVERSION CHARTS

Cup Measures

¼ cup	=	60ml
⅓ cup	=	80ml
½ cup	=	125ml
1 cup	=	250ml

Spoon Measures

¼ teaspoon	=	1.25ml
½ teaspoon	=	2.5ml
1 teaspoon	=	5ml
1 tablespoon	=	20ml

Dry Measures

Metric	Imperial
15g	½oz
30g	1oz
60g	2oz
90g	3oz
125g	4oz
155g	5oz
185g	6oz
220g	7oz
250g	8oz (½lb)
280g	9oz
410g	13oz
440g	14oz
470g	15oz
500g	16oz (1lb)
750g	24oz
1kg	32oz (2lb)

Liquid Measures

Metric	Imperial
30ml	1 fluid oz
60ml	2 fluid oz
100ml	3 fluid oz
125ml	4 fluid oz
150ml	5 fluid oz
190ml	6 fluid oz
250ml	8 fluid oz
300ml	10 fluid oz
500ml	16 fluid oz
600ml	20 fluid oz

Oven Temperatures

These oven temperatures are only a guide.
If using a fan forced oven set at about 20°C below stated temperatures.

	Gas		Electric	
	°C	°F	°C	°F
Very slow	120	250	125	250
Slow	150	300	150	300
Moderately slow	160	325	160–180	325–350
Moderate	180	350	180–200	375–400
Moderately hot	190	375	210–230	425–450
Hot	200	400	240–250	475–500
Very hot	230	450	260	525–550

GOURMET GARDEN®
HERBS & SPICES

Fresh Made Easy™

Fresh herbs and spices really make a difference to the flavour and quality of a meal, but during the week it's hard to find time to buy or prepare them. Here's a solution for all you busy cooks who don't want to miss out on flavour.

Gourmet Garden herbs are Australian grown then washed, chopped, blended and packed fresh. They contain no artificial flavours or colours and they last for 3 months in the fridge, so there's no wastage. The vibrant flavour, aroma and texture of your favourite fresh herbs and spices are only a squeeze away. They really are fresh herbs made easy for everyday cooking!

The Gourmet Garden range features 15 herbs and spices in tubes such as garlic, basil, coriander and chilli as well as the new Gourmet Garden Fresh Blends™, which are fresh chopped herbs and spices blended into the authentic varieties of Thai, Mediterranean, Moroccan and Indian.

For hundreds of delicious recipe ideas visit www.gourmetgarden.com

"Find Gourmet Garden in the fresh produce section of Coles"

SOME EASY USAGE TIPS:

BASIL: perfect in pastas, stir fries, dressings and soups.

CHILLI (AVAILABLE IN HOT & MILD CHILLI): adds spice to stir fries, curries, marinades & Mexican dishes.

CHIVES: boost the flavour of dressings, soups and potatoes.

CORIANDER: great in stir fries, curries and soups

DILL: a perfect accompaniment for seafood and dressings.

GARLIC (AVAILABLE IN REGULAR & CHUNKY GARLIC): great in everything from stir fries to pastas and curries to pizza.

GINGER: fantastic in stir fries, vegetables, curries and soups.

LEMON GRASS: adds exotic flavour to soups, curries and stir fries.

MINT: delicious with lamb and in dressings, sauces & dips.

OREGANO: perfect for pizzas, pastas, salads & meatballs.

PARSLEY: great in salads, pastas and sauces

ROSEMARY: fantastic on lamb & in salads and marinades.

ITALIAN HERBS: ideal for lasagne, meatballs, pizza & soups.

FRESH BLENDS™ MEDITERRANEAN: perfect in pastas, meatballs & dressings.

FRESH BLENDS™ INDIAN: fantastic for curries, marinades or dips.

FRESH BLENDS™ MOROCCAN: great in meatballs & couscous or as a marinade for lamb or chicken.

FRESH BLENDS™ THAI: perfect in stir fries, curries and dressings.

KAMBROOK
THE SMARTER CHOICE

Kambrook – A Great Australian Success Story

Kambrook was founded in 1972 by Frank Bannigan, an Australian inventor with an obsession for electrical appliances and a mission to bring the price of quality products within everyone's reach. Frank converted his home garage into a workshop and named the company after the street he lived in.

Kambrook set out to provide customers with practical products that would enhance everyday life. This philosophy quickly led to the invention of Kambrook's first major product – the four way power board, which Frank developed out of pure frustration – he did not have enough power points to test his products. It was a simple, low cost and effective solution that became a worldwide hit. The power board was quickly followed by another invention – the plug-in electric timer. This device was originally designed to test the life of every Kambrook appliance, without physically having to switch it on and off.

By the late 70s, Frank's inventive mind turned to a revolutionary new idea: the plastic kettle. With better heat insulation than metal, the new kettle was cheaper and much safer. It proved another major Australian success story with sales of more than 250,000 kettles in the first year.

Kambrook fast became a household name in Australia when it took on the sponsorship of one of Australia's all time favourite TV shows 'Young Talent Time' with the slogan, "It took Kambrook to think of it".

Another milestone came when Kambrook launched a range of home heaters. To demonstrate the new products' effectiveness, the company sent samples to Mawson station, Australia's research site in the world's most brutal testing environment - Antarctica.

Every Kambrook product is still built to the highest safety standards and performance levels, with extensive testing in the brand's Australian laboratories. It's the little extra features, like the tip-over switches on Kambrook heaters, that increase customer peace of mind.

The product range has now expanded into kitchen appliances, including slow cookers, frypans, rice cookers, food processors, blenders, mixers, toasters and kettles. The living room and bedroom are also catered for with vacuum cleaners, irons and electric blankets.

Today, every Kambrook product still lives up to Frank's original philosophy: affordable, quality appliances with far more features than you would expect at the price.

For more than 35 years Kambrook has been a name you can rely on.

www.kambrook.com.au

décor®

tellfresh® stackstore&pour™

Make the most of your storage space

Our new StackStore&Pour™ storers come in five handy sizes (550ml to 3.25 litres) that stack so neatly. Look for this value offer starter set containing all five sizes plus clip-on Tellfresh® tags, pencil and eraser. All sizes and tag sets are also available separately. No BPA. No anti-bacterial chemicals added.

Look for our distinctive circle pattern on the lid. www.decor.com.au
Designed and made in Australia   DC31/SW9

décor

thermoglass oven safe ™ NEW

Decor Thermoglass™ tempered glass dishes are designed for conventional oven-safe cooking. The rounded square shape ensures even heating. For microwaving, use the Microsafe® lids with steam-release vents. Close the vent for fridge or freezer storage. Look for the 7-piece Value Offer starter set including a trivet and Beverley Sutherland Smith recipe booklet. www.decor.com.au

Oven and **Microwave** and **Table** and **Freezer**

BUILT TO LAST LONGER

The ASKO story is a good one.

It started back in 1950 in Vara, Sweden, with an innovative young man's dream to build a washing machine for his mother to suit her every need. A unique, energy- and water efficient machine that would reflect a farmer's love for nature. One with superior cleaning performance and reliability that could heat water, spin and even boast durable, state-of-the-art stainless steel drums. A washing machine that would surpass even his meticulous mother's high standards. So he built a world-class facility right on the family farm – where it still stands today – and ASKO was born

Caring for design

Being Swedish means we are at the forefront of design. We believe that function and form are equally important. We believe our design must be timeless yet cutting edge. Simple to use yet complex enough to cope with all types of situations.

ASKO has always striven for the perfect balance of minimalism and clever appliances with a clear reference to reducing waste in all our design and production goals

Caring for quality

Quality for us is about durability and producing a product that will please you for a long time. It's about developing smart features that add life to our products while making them work better. It's about creating designs that subscribe to the Scandinavian principles of less is more, so our appliances will stand up to the changes of time. It's about outstanding performance, time after time after time.

The quality in our products is visible. Take a closer look at our dishwasher baskets; how sturdy they are; how they seamlessly glide in and out on stainless steel bearings; how flexible the racks are. Or if you are after a washing machine, we suggest you check our door seal solution, where the door seals directly to the drum without any unnecessary rubber bellows.

Simply, our products are built to last longer.

www.Asko.com.au

INDEX

apple
    apple puree, 63
    apple sponge with vanilla bean custard, 64
    crispy apple puffs, 68
    rhubarb and apple crumble, 124
Asian salad, 98
asparagus
    asparagus wrapped in bacon with cheese sauce, 50
    oyster mushroom asparagus salad, 74
    sautéed asparagus with poached egg, prosciutto and shaved parmesan, 26

banana
    banana fritters in butterscotch sauce, 48
    banana split with chocolate and caramel syrup, 128
    banana spring rolls with palm sugar caramel, 116
    caramelised banana crepes, 16
    caramelised bananas with brandied sauce, chocolate pecans and cream, 28
barberry rice, 19
battered prawns, 78
berry pancakes, 100
berry sauce, 72
bruschetta
    eggplant bruschetta, 86
    Italian bruschetta, 22
    mushroom and haloumi bruschetta, 62
    oyster shot and smoked salmon bruschetta, 90
bush honey chocolate fondue, 12
butter tarts, 56
butterscotch sauce, 48

cake, cherry slice, 136
calamari, spicy, and fresh herb salad, 114

INDEX

cannellini beans, fusillini with fresh tomato sauce and, 23

char siew, grilled, 67

cheese sauce, 50

cheesecake, eggnog, 52

cherry slice cake, 136

chhole chawal, 103

chicken
- almond and parmesan crusted chicken kiev, 123
- chicken pasta with mixed veggies, 79
- chicken snitzels with mash and mixed salad, 135
- grilled chicken with herbed breadcrumbs, 107
- honey soy chicken skewers, 98

chickpea, spicy, with puri, 139

chilli
- chilli mussels, 55
- dipping sauce, 14
- fillet steak with red wine, chilli & parmesan, 3
- prawns with chilli and ginger on ciabatta toast, 34

Chinese fish soup with noodles, 31

chocolate
- bush honey chocolate fondue, 12
- chocolate fondue with Bailey's cream, honeycomb and strawberries, 76
- chocolate sauce, 84
- chocolate self saucing pudding, 92
- pancakes with chocolate and walnuts, 60
- soft chocolate puddings, 88

chutney, 102

coconut custards, steamed, with lime, 32

coleslaw, 63

couscous, 98
- lemon, 47

cranberry jus, 51

INDEX

creamy delight, Persian, 20
crepes, banana, caramelised, 16
cucumber and yoghurt dip, 18
custard
    coconut custards with lime, 32
    vanilla bean, 64

dip, cucumber and yoghurt, 18
dipping sauce, 38
    chilli, 14

eggnog cheesecake, 52
eggplant
    eggplant bruschetta, 86
    eggplant crisps with herb and garlic dressing, 70

fettuccine, strawberry, 132
fillet steak with red wine, chilli & parmesan, 3
fish
    Chinese fish soup with noodles, 31
    crumbed fish fillets with tartare sauce, 27
    flavoured King George whiting with garlic sauce, 99
    Mediterranean fish and vegetables, 39
    tangy sauce grilled fish, 95
French onion soup, 54
fruit
    fruit kebab totem with ginger and honey yoghurt, 120
    fruit soup, 42
    seasonal stewed fruit, 40
fusillini with fresh tomato sauce and cannellini beans, 23

garlic prawns, 106

INDEX

glaze, red wine and chilli jam, 11

gluten free food

    gluten free linguine with mixed vegetables, 71

    gluten free pancakes, 4, 72

goats cheese with pizza, 2

haloumi

    mushroom and haloumi bruschetta, 62

    pan-fried, with sour dough crisps and radicchio and witlof salad, 94

    san choi bow with fried haloumi cheese, 66

halwa, 140

ham, pizza with, 2

herb and garlic dressing, 70

herb salad, 114

honey soy chicken skewers, 98

hummus bi tahina with warm turkish bread, 46

involtini

    spring pasta with, 131

    veal, 35

Italian affogato, 24

Italian bruschetta, homemade, 22

kangaroo fillet, 11

King George whiting with garlic sauce, 99

king prawns, stir fried in garlic and giner, 30

la tazza dolce, 108

lamb

    fig, fennel and butternut pumpkin lamb, 75

    lamb souzoukakia, 83

    seasoned lamb rack, 7

INDEX

lemon
- lemon couscous, 47
- lemon tart with strawberry salsa, 96
- lemon velvet, 44

loukoumades with honey and chocolate sauce, 84

meat and vegetable boulders with salsa, 111
meatballs, Moroccan, in spicy tomato sauce, 47
Mediterranean fish and vegetables, 39
Mediterranean vegies, chargrilled and sautéed, 82
mocha sundae, 112
Moroccan meatballs in spicy tomato sauce, 47
mushrooms
- bbq pork with snow peas, enoki mushrooms and rice noodles, 67
- mushroom and fennel risotto, 91
- mushroom and haloumi bruschetta, 62
- oyster mushroom asparagus salad, 74
- swiss brown, stuffed with caramelised onions and blue cheese, 6

mussels
- chilli mussels, 55
- wine, cooked in, 58

noodles
- bbq pork with snow peas, enoki mushrooms and rice noodles, 67
- Chinese fish soup with noodles, 31
- won ton noodle soup, 15

oyster
- oyster pies, 115
- oyster shot and smoked salmon bruschetta, 90
- salsa oysters with cucumber sandwiches, 122

INDEX

pancakes
    berry, 100
    chocolate and walnuts, with, 60
    gluten free buttermilk, with ice-cream and a wild berry and chambord sauce, 72
    gluten free low carb pancakes, 4
    pancake delight, 80
    potato pancake stack, 43

parfait, strawberry, 8

pasta
    chicken pasta with mixed veggies, 79
    fusillini with fresh tomato sauce and cannellini beans, 23
    gluten free linguine with mixed vegetables, 71
    spring pasta with involtini, 131
    strawberry fettuccine, 132

Persian creamy delight, 20

pies, oyster, 115

pizza
    yeast free, with ham, goats cheese, rocket and basil, 2

pork
    bbq pork with snow peas, enoki mushrooms and rice noodles, 67
    fennel seed crusted pork loin, 63

potato
    dry roasted potato scallops, 27
    mashed native sweet potato, 11
    potato bhajiya and chutney, 102
    potato cubes, fried, 7
    potato gratin, 51

prawns
    battered prawns, 78
    garlic prawns, 106
    prawns in coconut milk, 127
    prawns with chilli and ginger on ciabatta toast, 34

INDEX

    spiced coconut prawns, 10

    stir fried king prawns in garlic and ginger, 30

puddings

    chocolate self saucing pudding, 92

    soft chocolate puddings, 88

puri, 139

red wine

    fillet steak with, 3

    red wine and chilli jam glaze, 11

rhubarb and apple crumble, 124

rice, barberry, 19

risotto

    mushroom and fennel risotto, 91

    squid ink risotto, 59

salads

    Asian salad, 98

    fresh herb salad, 114

    oyster mushroom asparagus salad, 74

    radicchio and witlof salad, 94

    rocket, beetroot, feta and roasted pine nuts, 7

    salad dressing, 63

salmon

    oyster shot and smoked salmon bruschetta, 90

    salmon fillet, 119

    salmon with Asian greens on a bed of chive mash, 87

salsa oysters with cucumber sandwiches, 122

san choi bow with fried haloumi cheese, 66

sauces

    berry sauce, 72

    butterscotch sauce, 48

INDEX

    cheese sauce, 50
    fresh tomato sauce, 23
    garlic sauce, 99
    spicy tomato sauce, 47
    tartare, 27

sausage crostini, Tuscan, 130
scotch fillet, pan fried, 91
sheera, 104
soup
    French onion soup, 54
    fruit soup, 42
    pumpkin and sweet potato soup, 118
    traditional Croatian semolina dumpling soup, 134
    won ton noodle soup, 15

spring pasta with involtini, 131
spring rolls
    banana, with palm sugar caramel, 116
    Vietnamese, 14
squid
    squid ink risotto, 59
    Thai style squid salad, 126
steak
    fillet steak with red wine, chilli & parmesan, 3
    mock t-bone, with potato pancake stack and tomato crown, 43
    pan fried scotch fillet, served on a bed of mushroom and fennel risotto, 91

stewed fruit, 40
strawberries
    lemon tart with strawberry salsa, 96
    strawberry and mint salsa, 116
    strawberry fettuccine, 132
    strawberry parfait, 8

INDEX

sweet potato
- mashed, 11
- pumpkin and sweet potato soup, 118

swiss brown mushrooms stuffed with caramelised onions and blue cheese, 6

tartare sauce, 27

tarts
- butter tarts, 56
- lemon tart with strawberry salsa, 96

Thai style squid salad, 126

tiramisu, 36

tomato
- fresh tomato sauce, 23
- roast tomato, 27
- spicy tomato sauce, 47
- tomato crown, 43
- tomatoes' pottage, 138

traditional Croatian semolina dumpling soup, 134

turkey, stuffed, roast, with cranberry jus, 51

Tuscan sausage crostini, 130

vanilla bean custard, 64

veal involtini, 35

vegetables
- chicken pasta with mixed veggies, 79
- gluten free linguine with mixed vegetables, 71
- meat and vegetable boulders with salsa, 111
- Mediterranean vegies, chargrilled and sautéed, 82
- zesty vegetable tempura and herbed rice, 110

Vietnamese rolls, 38

Vietnamese spring rolls, 14

won ton noodle soup, 15

INDEX

yoghurt
- cucumber and yoghurt dip, 18
- fruit kebab totem with ginger and honey yoghurt, 120

zesty vegetable tempura and herbed rice, 110

★ Great Aussie Cook Off - Top 8 Cookbook – OUT EARLY 2010

★ Auditions now open for 2010 season, for more information visit www.colescookoff.com.au

★ Watch the families cooking their recipes online at www.colescookoff.com.au